SUBCONCIOUSLY UNCONSCIOUS

by

MARCOS GRAY

UBCONSCIOUSLY UNCONSCIOUS
Copyright © 2011

ISBN-10 is 1461062896
And
ISBN-13 is 978-1461062899

Published by
MIDNIGHT EXPRESS BOOKS
POBox 69
Berryville AR 72616
(870) 210-3771
http://MidnightExpressBooks.com
Email: MEBooks1@yahoo.com

Praise For Marcos Gray's
SUBCONSCIOUSLY UNCONSCIOUS

"I began reading *Subconsciously Unconscious* with a notion that I already had a good level of awareness, yet I was surprised at all of the things that I didn't know. It showed me that no one is immune from continually growing with respects to their knowledge. I would recommend this book to those, who like me, are always eager to increase in their knowledge."

Steven H.

"I was amazed at how so many of the things *Subconsciously Unconscious* discussed, but I was uninformed about them until I read this book. I never really thought about them, or the way we had been taught, and the significance that makes to our future as African Americans. It's amazing at how purported facts are taught as truth in our school systems and how we believe every word without ever considering the truth of the story. I found this book to be very enlightening and would recommend it to anyone inquisitive enough to know about truthful account's of American History."

Cordell W.

"I was grateful to learn of so many different things that I was unconscious of. It shocked me just how blatant a lot of the things in *Subconsciously Unconscious* were really happening right before our eyes, yet we fail to ever really look at it. I definitely will read it again and support the message of this book. It is worth reading at least twice."

Reginald B.

DEDICATION

I would like to dedicate this book to my Lord Yeshua ("Jesus") Christ because of His allowance of me to not only survive unconsciousness, but to allow for me to obtain a degree of consciousness. The journey was (is) tumultuous, but I'm confident that He'll allow for me to reach my destination.

I would also like to dedicate this to my mother for her continued love and support, even when it seemed that I was unlovable or worthy of support.

I also dedicate this to my step father and though he's passed; his words for me to, "stop looking on the ground because there isn't anything there, but to walk with my head up." These words have kept me focused on what may be ahead.

I also MUST dedicate this to my "brothers" Antonio and Michael because even though they aren't blood relatives, they have ALWAYS tried to instill in me the idea that greatness must be developed and sought after constantly in order to be attained.

I also must dedicate this to my Lord for the same reason I've acknowledged Him-His faithfulness to me.

ACKNOWLEDGEMENT

I must acknowledge all of the esteemed people whose research has helped me to substantiate and simplify these facts. Their insights were invaluable.

I must ESPECIALLY emphasize the research of J.A. Rogers in his completed works, *"Africa's Gift to America"* and *"Sex and Race vol. 3."* His insight helped expose past president's unknown, yet documented ideas about "African Americans" which aren't widely known.

I must also thank and acknowledge Mr. And Mrs. Huddleston for their patience, efficiency and professionalism, because even at times when I failed to demonstrate those traits, their loyalty to my endeavor has helped me give birth to these ideas, which had been lingering for years; I thank you BOTH.

I also must acknowledge my Lord for the exact same reason I dedicated this book to Him; for His faithfulness.

INTRODUCTION

In introducing "Subconsciously Unconscious," it simply is my goal to help all who read it realize that its geared towards ideals which can potentially facilitate our development in the future in a more productive, positive fashion. We must evolve from the present abysmal conditions that we suffer from. We have to become conscious of our heritage, strength, and also our potential. Dr. Asa Hilliard (psychologist and historian of African descent) stated, "We Africans... have not viewed our problem holistically. After years of living under conditions of extreme oppression, we have settled for limited definitions of our problem." One of these examples is in the fact that we've considered ourselves WHATEVER this country chooses to call us: from niggers, to black, to colored, to negro, finally to "African American."

I prefer the terminology native African. This is where our ancestry originates and since this society persists in making us feel separated from the Caucasian citizens in this country, we should demand recognition of our ancestry in stronger terms. Why are we not simply American citizens if we're born here? If Caucasians whose ancestry began in England or Ireland aren't called English American, or Irish American, then why is our ancestry isolated and used in our descriptions as a citizen? It seems clear that the fact that we're born over here is irrelevant, so we are ostracized, with the real idea or belief, that we're not true American citizens. We're simply "African Americans."

Dr. Hilliard continues: "First, we must see ourselves as an African people, or we will be unable to develop this critical frame. Second, we must understand not only the role that white supremacy has played in our subjugation, but also the role we ourselves have played by not practicing self determination in our struggle to counter the MAAFA." (This is Ki-Wahili term that means disaster or as Marimba Ani has conceptualized it to mean the African Holocaust of Eurasian enslavement/Colonialism).

We can all agree how education is vital to the elevation of any individual's success on a massive scale. Dr. John Henrik Clarke stated," education is one of the most sensitive areas in the life of a people. Its role is to be honest and true and to tell people where they have been and what they are." Information in this book will demonstrate just how systematically we've been giving false information, with regards to those two criteria of education according to Dr. Clarke. A true education engages the conscious of the people, and this in turn will potentially alter the current devastation that we see in our communities.

I challenge you to read this, not only with your eyes open, but with your conscious open. Hopefully this will inspire you to begin to grow mentally and in tune with the accomplishments of Native Africans in America. Such information of an individual's past has the capability to lead them to a productive future. May God bless you and us in this struggle to stop allowing for ourselves to be subconsciously unconscious.

CONTENTS

CHAPTER 1
How Far We've Come

It goes beyond any argument that Native Africans have excelled in almost every facet of life: including politics. However, there exists a large portion of the Native African politician's who have become, or always were indifferent to the people of his/her heritage. They exist solely for the purpose of themselves and have no real concern for the plight of their heritage. They use their political status as only a catalyst to further their careers and increase their personal wealth. They make even the most prejudiced Caucasian seem compassionate to our current state.

In general, the position of government seems to be to take as much from one group of people and give it to another; unfortunately it seems that it's the poor who suffer and the wealthy that benefit. Of course the Caucasians have deceptive politicians also, but the fact that they have over 400 years of a head start and they don't have as many "opposing factors" against them, they can afford to have a questionable politician in their communities. Yet, even in their deception, their politicians do not blatantly disregard their heritage, and even in the off-chance that they do they have multiple organization's to minimize the damage that may be done to them because of disloyalty to their heritage.

We seem to have none (or few) Native African politicians who are willing to confront, let alone rectify, the wrongs committed against "their" community.

The only "confrontation" seems to come during election season and after the elections are done with, any remedies are seldom brought. No consequence for the actions or in-action is reaped, except for maybe a failure to be re-elected or elected; most of the time it seems like "the lesser of two evils." The corruptible Native Africans in politics seem to monopolize the field and so regardless to which one we choose, it seems very much like we have chosen the same. It is as if our consciousness of the issues is always distorted. Our present political leaders of African heritage must be converted to that of concern for their people, because we cannot realistically expect for any one of any other heritage to TRULY desire our elevation in society. If they're unwilling to do that they need to be removed.

It seems improbable that our current "leaders" will reform themselves or their methods apart from an external influence, (voters). These selfish beings seem to be in collusion with the societal methods of robbing and extorting our communities of their money, values and all out hope of a productive future, apart from entertaining society. It's disheartening that we've been afflicted with such unconscious people for so long as we have been. Their faces may be of the same complexion as ours, but their souls and hearts have been tainted by dollar signs, even at the expense of our communities well being or their need to please others at our expense.

They fail to realize that the same hands that seemingly helped them rise will be the same hand to manufacture their fall by placing blame on them to save one of their own, (i.e. Colin Powell). Those who treat politics and morality as separate will never understand either. This society's prejudices and our politicians of African lineage seems to be un-noticed in their collusion towards our communities and it's largely due to a sub-conscious unconsciousness instilled into Native Africans through media and its propaganda, which manipulates our culture and western society in large. Society fails to realize that politicians are to have their constituent's best interest at heart, but mostly they have only themselves in mind.

We would do much better as a people if we realized that we owe no loyalty to any one party in the political sphere, perhaps if we placed more interest and focus on GOD and what we could accomplish we'd be much better off. It seems to not be on anyone's agenda to rectify the discrepancies in the numbers at which Native Africans in this country are being incarcerated. According to the U.S. Department of Justice and the U.S. Census Bureau "African American's" make up of 59.5% of the prison population, yet only 12. 9% of the United States total population. Yet, Caucasian males make up of 66% of the U.S. population, and 1% of the prison population. These statistics are not as surprising as they seem, because it's played out all over the country.

Sadly, the unconscious fail to realize the deliberate designs against Native Africans and it's evident in many ways and has been so for centuries. One of their "subtle" ways is the fact that prosecution for "rock" cocaine will get an individual years in prison, yet it's counter-part powder will reap minimal, (if any), jail time. The primary cause of this is because the "rock" is mainly found in "African American communities," and powder is found mainly in Caucasian communities. No other logic can excuse it; in fact they've recently begun to look at this disproportionate form of sentencing. Schemes like this of legislature have to be noticed by Native African politicians, yet they feel as if they don't affect them, so it's of no consequence to them one way or another.

This is not only indicative of unconsciousness, but a lack of conscience. I'm sure I'm not the only one to recognize such subliminal messages given to our youth, who are being "forced" to view those things as reality. This creates a wave of young minds believing (falsely) that they're expendable. All we have to do is look at the entertainment industry and what it speaks to us about what it thinks about us. Before I go further I must express I have only admiration for the actress Halle Berry and my observations are not to be taken as an attack on her or anyone for that matter. With that said, I will speak a truth many may not have thought about or agree with, but the truth stays the same regardless to who accepts it. Hollywood depreciated the dozens of movies she'd starred in prior to the 2002 "Monsters Ball." This role was in my opinion, one of the most disrespectful to our women (with the exception of pornography) to be filmed. The fact that it was a Caucasian as her counter-part is not the main issue I have, but the sheer tastelessness in which it was filmed.

I must express that I'm in no way a separatist, racist or segregationist, because there is only one race-human. Yet, when one group of people suffer from superiority complexes, and we Native Africans suffer an inferiority complex on such a massive scale that it manifests itself in ALL areas in which we take up. To further add insult to her "Oscar winning performance," the characters lacked depth. Here is a tale of a Native African woman who is single handedly raising her son and the father's in prison and she starts a relationship with one of the guards at the prison her husband is condemned to die in.

I haven't chosen to use Ms. Berry or the industry as a scapegoat for our unconsciousness, but as an example of how no one took issue with THAT being the role for which she received an award celebrating her talent. We must be honest, the entertainment industry is a monetary lead entity and it will exploit whoever allows for themselves to be exploited. Thank GOD for stronger sisters like Angela Basset who refused that role. Monetary gains for some may come to Native Africans, but at what expense? It isn't enough money in existence to demean and justify our being demeaned by the entertainment industry, or any other industry for that matter, with that being said, that is all that the "entertainment" industry is it will exploit us as well as anyone. There isn't enough compensation in existence to justify what we're allowing to be done to ourselves. And without consciousness, we've become content on behaving EXACTLY how society has groomed for us to be. This inferiority complex is one of the most pervasive attributes in Native Africans in this western culture.

We see this further demonstrated by the lack of outrage of our communities at the incessant examples of police brutality being committed against our youth. This has been a part of our life for as long as we've been in this country, yet the recent excessiveness of it and the short term anger over it only comes from the respective community in which the violence occurred. We rarely have any Native African politicians speaking about it, and if they do, they don't act on it. We can be sure that because of the further demonstration of our lives as being devalued by this western society we will continue to be misled.

This shown through our prosecutions 5 times more than our Caucasian counter-parts and the systematic murder of our males, by either the implementation of the death penalty or just the blatant murder of them in the streets. This is according to the Office of Professional Standards and the Department of Justice. Our subconsciousness reflects that we too are in the belief that our life has no real value. When this is the culture that teaches us, it's evident that we'll begin to and continue to, behave as we are. It's demonstrated by our turning our hatred and frustration inward on ourselves because of a hopeless feeling propagated by a nation, whose hypocrisy is globally known.

It began with the document titled U.S. Constitution. This has the greatest potential to be a just document overall, however it clearly is not applied in a fashion in which many of our communities can feel it's affects. It claims to hold dear, "truth, justice and the American way," but too often it delivers lies and injustice all caused by (or mostly) by racism. The Native Africans feel this in the worst way, unless they are in possession of enough money to buy the alleged "freedoms and rights" they're supposed to have the fortune of owning if they were born here.

This nationwide practice of sending Native Africans to jail more frequently than other people in this country, for longer than any other, is blatantly demonstrative of how we're valued by society. As of June 30, 2007 the Bureau of Justice reported that for each 100,000 males in this country "African American" males have 4,619 men in prison, while Latinos comprise of only 1,747 men in jail. The Caucasian men however, consist of only 773 men in jail. It is ironic that "Native African" men comprise of 12.9% of the population as of June 2005, but make up of over 50% of the prison population. And as of January 2007, 91% of men in prison for drug offenses were "African Americans," though the same report showed that Caucasians use them more frequently.

President Bill Clinton is remembered with such affections by people of African lineage, but the 1994 "3 strikes law" was potentially one of the most damaging pieces of legislation to decimate the "African American" communities. If one is unconscious exactly what the "3 strikes law" is, simply put it's the legal authority to sentence an individual to life in prison for a act as trivial as stealing a piece of bread if he's had 2 prior convictions, whether or not if the crimes were violent. And who do you think suffers the most from that legislation?

I am not condoning any criminal acts, but I am against any penalty inflicted on us with more severity than it's inflicted on others for the same act. I don't desire for my words to be misrepresented: all ethnicities have their short comings, so no one group will be indicted by me. It would be irresponsible for me to condemn any one group based on the behavior of the worst of their kind. I abhor evil perpetrated by any, but I ABSOLUTELY despise evil against us.

These injustices, which are so blatant, ought to cause for all of its citizens to be enraged by it, not just the "African American" community. We believe the U.S. Constitution gives us these protections, but more than often we are shown no consideration, with respects to the "life, liberty, pursuit of happiness" we believe we have. It's more elusive than the concept of a utopia which has evaded humanity since its beginnings.

No man can place a chain around the ankle of another without finding the other end tied to his own neck. I feel that no greater crime is committed than to teach our kids that unconsciousness is acceptable. Believe it or not, we are in this together as a people, despite the fact that many choose to ignore the crimes committed against us in the name of justice. All are affected to some degree, or at least we ought to be. It's obvious that unconsciousness will help breed complacency in our communities, and we all see the results of that. We will never obtain the respect of others, if we don't respect ourselves. If we truly love ourselves, we will hate the ones who seek to bring about our destruction, or at the very least, we will seek to undo it whether it's physical, psychological or economical.

Consciousness gives us a chance to do better, but unconsciousness yields the exact opposite result. For those in the belief that they're conscious, we bear the responsibility of enlightening those who are unconscious. A good indicator of unconsciousness in us is that those who feel some logic in placing "national pride" as their primary concern. Nationality means nothing when it conflicts with our heritage, which so often it has. Not to mention this very nation often down plays our citizenship anyway. If our people fail to realize that nationality can be changed, it can't be deemed as important as ones heritage. Heritage isn't optional; you can't wake up and decide that you're going to become another ethnicity, no matter how much you can afford to pay to bleach your skin. So, in reality, nationality is NOT more important than ones heritage.

I don't mean to sound "anti-American," because as previously stated, this country has the greatest potential for many, but its racist inner workings have been so corrupted with hypocrisy that even the U.S. Constitution contradicts with the various states, their own arbitrary laws. And this causes for injustice to persist in its many forms that we witness today. I don't wish to appear hostile or prejudiced myself, but this country needs to be called on its prejudices.

The fundamental concepts of Native African consciousness is that we reject all systems that wishes to treat us as aliens in the country that we virtually built. I can't fail to mention it so often minimizes our basic human dignities. There is no shame to be attributed to us for speaking for any type of "awakening" of our people. Society appreciates our unconsciousness, it also benefits from it.

There's no role we under value so much as the duty of being conscious even though it's continually proven elusive to us. If we refuse to walk away from toxic influences, they will inevitably destroy us further than they currently are.

The scariest thing is that the cruelest lies are told to us subconsciously. There exist at least three things necessary for our survival: to know what and who we ought to believe, to know what we are to desire, to know what we are to do in order to obtain it. We must consider our posterity; we were not born to live like beasts, but to follow virtue and knowledge. Without it being taught to our children, we will continue to see genocidal characteristics. Obviously, with our information being faulty, this means our judgment will be as well.

We will continue to see our communities ravaged. This devastation caused by unconsciousness. How we live is often far from how we should and as long as we abandon what we need to do for what we want, we'll continue to yield to negative influences and reap the same results. There is a strength in knowing who we truly are; strong and courageous, living, thriving in the midst of a racist, adversarial system, with an onslaught of negative designs. We still have the potential to overcome them and often some of us do, but the numbers of those that do so are not nearly enough.

May we not take pride in wealth and the illusion that it offers, because that isn't indicative of consciousness, which is by far more important. Our cultural responsibilities will aid us in growing more conscious. Many judge externally, by either prestige or wealth, but that is error because consciousness is a thing to be sought, it can't be bought. It must be discovered.

A physiological fact of our bodies is that the more frequent we use a specific muscle, it gradually strengthens, develops and enlarges itself. This simply means that it will deteriorate and weaken from a lack of usage. This means that over a period of time its capacities and capabilities will fail to live up to its fullest potential.

We need in our consciousness a usage of our brain (mentality), a constant strengthening. Without it, we will continue to see catastrophic deeds occurring in our communities at the same or increased levels at which we are seeing. It's unquestionable that unconsciousness is easier than consciousness, because it takes the shortest route to everything, but there is no bliss in ignorance ESPECIALLY when we suffer so constantly and on so many levels because of our unconsciousness.

We often follow destructive propaganda so blindly. The preconceived opinions influence us so greatly that it brings unconsciousness into our minds and plants it as truth. The irrationality of this perceived "truth" that we hold so dear is detrimental to us on a multitude of levels. The "African Americans" in this society have over 400 years of dieting on misinformation. We've been made to see the world and its history through another's eyes and this has been occurring for centuries. This makes it hard for us to realize our true worth. Society in America has in large part caused our genocidal mentality and then Perpetuating stereotypes of us as being naturally criminal, thus making us the constant scapegoat for all (or most) ills in this society.

Our history has been so distorted that most are unaware that they are being denied a glimpse of our value and historical contribution to this continent, no, to the WORLD! Slavery was only a part of our history; the rest has been misplaced systematically. It is a constant attempt at "white washing" us out of the annals of the history books, but fortunately we are not dependant on their veracity to know who we are, although some of their scholars recognize our value. Sir Godfrey Higgins wrote in "Anacalypsis Vol. 1 pg. 235; "we have found the black complexion or something relating to it whenever we approach to the origins of nations." If we could instill this into the consciousness of our children, we'd reap better behavior from them.

Our unconsciousness knows nothing greater than itself, but consciousness instantly realizes many of the devices set up against it (and us), for what purpose. Whenever we neglect instilling consciousness in our youth, we make it easier to disregard it in their (and our) adulthood. Our individual lives are not as important as the continuation of our heritage, but on a level greater than entertainment, pleasure and, the likes. We are in possession of a GOD given desire to see our children grow in a world where they'll be treated and received better than we have been, by and large, by society.

I must re-emphasis that without us making any efforts at creating a "better world," it will NEVER be brought into fruition. I'm not falsely stating prejudice would completely leave this Northern American continent, but as long as we demonstrate unconsciousness to the schemes perpetrated against us, we will always have other people believing that we're inferior to them; no one is as interested in our preservation as we ought to be. I'm aware of, and proud of, some advancements we have obtained, but there still exists a darker reality beyond the fictitious "American dream" and its sunlit society; sadly we've assisted in our own denigration by believing and feeding on the false images given to us. As far as we've come, we've only just begun.

Subconsciously Unconscious

CHAPTER 2
Blinded Vision

"Too long have others spoken for us, we wish to plead our own cause." John Brussworm was the owner of those words and the first owner and publisher of an African American newspaper in the 1800's. He demonstrated an insight which is just as true today as they were when he spoke them. We have many more publishing entities operated by African Americans, but we still are being fed a diet of negativity thru their media outlet. The major difference between the 19th century and today's 21st century is that we have more money in our communities but unfortunately this is spent on cosmetics, cars, jewelry and a plethora of potentially damaging items. Billions are spent on just those three mentioned and yet we're content that even though it's more money in our hands, we're STILL, just as poor as we've been in times past.

Fact: the public school system distributes more money to suburban districts than to inner city school districts. Having an inept schooling system from a toddler to teenage years, this is a main catalyst for the misdirection and its one of the greatest hindrances and a major cause for why we lack consciousness, we are to be adamant that our children receive the same privileges and opportunities as those in districts where their inhabitants make two or three times as that of those in our urban communities. This in turn causes their school districts to reap continued benefits (programs, computers, books, etc.)

The justification of this is because those suburban district inhabitants have higher property taxes, more businesses bringing in more revenue, so this implies that the allocation of millions more for their schools is justified and that the less fortunate are receiving what they deserve, basically nothing. In conscious eyes, we see that it is primarily African Americans, Latinos, and poor Caucasians being disadvantaged. So, is not necessarily only a "race" issue, but a division of classes. But the poorer tends to be people of African lineage.

In 1980 250,000 more African American males were in college than in prison, now only 20 plus years later the prison population of those same out numbers the collegiate African American male by almost the same 250,000 (183,000). The shift has been so drastic and devastating to us all; in fact the Department of Justice stated that if the current trend isn't stopped, one in three African American males will be incarcerated. That ought to be enough to cause the most callous of us to be forced to wonder how we really feel about our heritage.

I believe that we deserve a fairness guaranteed to us by a constitution that we fought and died for, believing that a freedom would be ours. It was promised by this country's "founding fathers." The same tyranny they believed they suffered at the hands of the British Empire (King George), they had no qualms about inflicting it on African slaves 1000 fold. Our fighting for the then new America proved that we would be much worse off after the revolutionary war than before it. Once we solidified a win for the new America, we were subjected to more horrific trans-Atlantic journeys by the American Caucasian.

A catalyst (a big one), was the local legislation in 1773 flat out refused the British merchants from landing, on the Boston Harbor because the British monopolized the tea trade. The Americans were tired of being taxed excessively, hence the slogan "no taxation without representation." They decided to rebel, rather revolt. The American Caucasians dressed as Native Americans and threw 342 chests of tea into the sea, after beating the crew up. More riots in American colonial locations discouraged the British efforts to bring in more tea.

This cowardly act has been hailed as an act of true heroism. The history books fail to mention that the Americans intended to blame this on the Native Americans. "In plain language, therefore, it was the profit from the sale of Africans and the wealth they produced that was the underlying cause of the Revolution, in short had there been no Africa, the U.S. might still be attached to Britain...thus the wealth gained from the sale of Africans labor not only laid the foundation of Americas commerce, but the attempt to deprive Britain of the benefit of the slave trade was the direct cause of the Revolution." (Africa's gift to America by J.A. Rogers)

However, if African Americans become frustrated at excessive police brutality, injustices or all around aggravation by the prejudicial treatment by this American society, it's hailed as criminality or terrorism. The subconscious message is that the Caucasian American has at their disposal an aura of justification for whatever it is that they do; no matter how cowardice it is or dastardly. Yet, our acts of rebellion are depicted as violent and unjustified. I can't judge any individuals choice to riot, but history shows how frequently "uprisings" occur, but it's called a riot if African Americans do it.

I believe that in such acts, we fail to consider what would yield the best results, but frustration is a strong motivation. The fact of this country's history displays the character of its so called "founding fathers" and modern political figures in this land demonstrate similarities to them. The signers of the Declaration of Independence had all been land owners and plantation owners and business owners. In fact, one could not hold political office without being a part of this aristocracy, but not much has really changed on that note.

John Hancock had been involved in the slave trade. Thomas Jefferson is well known for having many slave born children by his slave women. Yet, this didn't stop him from claiming that "the orangutan preferred black women to those of his species." (Sex and Race vol. 3 by J.A. Rogers). He also said," black men were void of mental endowment." One can suppose that he himself was an orangutan, considering his well documented affinity for our black girls. The typical hypocritical behavior

18

of ancient figures in this country's past is still shown by present politicians.

These are individuals that this country would have us to show honor, but at the slightest accusation made against one of us goes into the heart of the nation as any indictment on us all, not to mention the vilification of our accused and subconsciously us.

First American president, (then general) Washington saw he must use the "negro or run the risk of losing the Revolutionary war" and he wrote Col. Henry Lee, December 10, 1775 stating, "success will depend on which side can arm the negro faster...negroes were accepted in such numbers now that General Schuyler wrote "is it consistent with the sons of freedom to trust their all to be defended by slaves" (Africa's Gift to America pg 220). If it were not for the African slaves, the American society we all are familiar with would quite potentially still be under the British Empires rule.

Those slaves who fought for the beast which would devour them and their children for centuries were unaware of the depths of the Americans deceit. The African slaves (present lineage included) have an innate quality to believe in the best of people, even if they have done injustices to us (them) in the past. Today, we have no excuse for our unconsciousness. We have for too long allowed for materialism to mislead us into thinking that we've obtained liberty. Even with agreeing with so much negativity about our own people propagated by this American culture.

One of these instances is the fact that we've taken one of the most reprehensible words in existence and tried to make it "cultural." The "nigger/nigga" word has its foundation in 19th century racism and no amount of usage will justify it. Though we have more pressing matters to address, this words usage in our communities still needs to be ceased. Those reading may be unwilling to change their ideals about acceptable conduct, because of a notion about change being uncomfortable. Uncomfortable people complain because of a notion that the way they're living is good enough as it is. Fear of growth is allowing for a complacent mentality at being unconscious.

We need to be protectors of our children and our women because our future depends on it. Too often many of us are willing to live for nothing, but what are we willing to die for? Those who deem themselves proud African Americans ought to be visionaries for the cause of our survival. Not a visionary for a new clothing line or in the entertainment industry but a visionary for the elevation of our next generation's consciousness. All the false illusions of liberty that we view constantly dangled over our psyche, yet it is merely an altered form of slavery. We must learn to become satisfied only if the things we suffer for survive and become a benefit to our future heritage. If not, the suffering is in vain.

How many of us can look at his brother and see his pain and not be moved by it? Sadly, we have bred too many callous people in our communities. All of us have a capacity for greatness, but not all of us desire to obtain it. The Native Africans in America have never had easy lives; negativity clouds our minds and clouded minds are dimmed and dimmed minds are unconscious of what's usually in our (its) midst. We all know the wounds of injustice and suffering linger longer than is admitted, but we must not allow our hurt to turn into hate or anger, which can turn into violence, this can cause for us to be unfocused on the task at hand.

And the primary task is the awakening of our consciousness. We don't need to adopt old tactics to try to awaken ourselves, but we can use newly acquired social and economic status that some of us enjoy; it's our responsibility. We're collectively to bear special burdens being born what we were born as. We are required to start behind square one, which is a main cause that so many of us fall victim to the negative devices that this society propagates even before we're able to compete on an academic level.

The falsehoods being taught to us, such as our hair is too thick, or our skin is too dark have brainwashed us into denying our beauty. We should disregard the concepts of beauty that the westernized countries try to sell us. These long reaching ideals deprive us of true freedom. Freedom is defined as "independence liberation, and privilege, the right to choose the direction of our lives without allowing society to negatively influence

21

us." Freedom is an escape from the stereotypes that keep us shackled to lies. Many "African-Americans" attempt to justify dye of blond color to their hair, or blue and green contact and bleaching skin as merely as fashionable. This is no more fashionable than the early Caucasian settlers in America dressing themselves as Native Americans was heroic.

Regardless to what people record in the history books, it is a well established fact that "He who wins the war, writes the story." Truth is often of no consequence. Our people who justify their hatred of their God given attributes demonstrate unconsciousness on a plane so detrimental to themselves, that it is almost suicidal on a mental level. Who decided that blue eyes and blond hair is the epitome of beauty? Who decided thinner lips and noses and lighter skin was more attractive? We will get to that later. We are not to compare ourselves with others, because it enslaves us to enemies which only exist in our minds. We have enough enemies. The most ignorant person would concede that those who look like that established the standards of "beauty."

Sadly, we've fell for this without hardly any resistance. Are we so dissatisfied with our physical attributes that we acclimate to their ideals of beauty so readily? I don't mean to criticize Caucasians, no more than I wish to Native Africans, but I do wish to critique the harmful patterns that exist in our communities. They need to see the beauty of their untapped potential which resides in them. This is a job too large for any one individual to accomplish by themselves. Our areas across the globe are often battle zones and often we're the perpetrators of the atrocities.

It is long pass due that we stop discussing the problems of our communities and start actively seeking the remedy of the problems. Unconsciousness will only allow us to see what's right before us, but the things which lay a little farther off will continue to stay out of our reach and potentially damage us further than we've seen. It is unquestionable that we've made advancements in every field, but we've demonstrated no trust in ourselves to enlighten our children. We've placed our most prized assets (our children) into the hands of those who willfully diminish our roles in civilization by teaching half truths or false versions in the construction of civilization.

Our children need to be taught that we haven't been under subjugation by the other "races" of people forever. In fact, prior to the slave trade we had a celebrated history as Kings, Queens, Pharaohs and Emperors and according to Caucasian author H. G. Wells, he said of his European ancestors that "away in the forests of Europe were the blond Nordic people-hunters and herdsmen A lowly race, the primitive civilizations saw very little of this race before 1500 A.D. (A Short History of the World).

I don't quote that to try to isolate the Europeans for verbal attack, because anyone who is able to raise themselves up to such a global dominance deserves respect. I did quote it to demonstrate that despite what this society's conscious attempts at making the important roles of history be solely relegated to Europeans; they were not.

The substandard housing and poverty we suffer from in masses today has helped nourish the seeds of unconsciousness and this has been the life that most of us have known since the supposed emancipation of slaves. We need to build and construct independent institutions and formations that will ensure our survival and enhance our children's quality of life in this hostile society. This will mean re-inventing our present perception and consider each of our endeavors. We must ask whether they will help or hinder our collective advancement as a people.

We have too many entities and organizations against us, so we definitely are in need of people within our heritage making it a priority to assist our future generations for children.

Each other heritage, the Jewish, the Chinese and the Native American are praised at their efforts at liberating and making the conditions of their life better, regardless to what method they use. We have continually been told that we should just forget the past abuse we've suffered and accept assimilation of ourselves into the "American way of life."

This should cause the conscious mind to seek out the unconscious minds in order to help keep our posterity relevant. It will be our conscious thoughts or our unconscious decisions which will mold our lives and the lives of our children. We must educate ourselves how to obtain wisdom from the injustices we face, but not the negative from them. We native Africans, rather the conscious ones, know that our life is more than a struggle; it's warfare. Fighting for our rights which are denied regularly, plus our young men who are being incarcerated in record numbers, not to mention the rate at which they're murdered. Not to mention our women who are disrespected by everybody on the planet, but by us more vehemently.

No one will respect us as men if we fail to show respect to our women. As we stand right now, do we deserve it? These truths may seem unacceptable to some right now, but the quicker they come to the realization of our situation, the quicker they will be willing to at least attempt to rectify it. It's indisputable that truths which stir consciousness will never fade and should be the desire of all Native Africans, but how few seek it. There's nothing stronger than consciousness, yet often we are weakened by our willful ignorance of it.

Our entire American voyage and the mistreatment with it ought to always be in our subconscious, but it's as if we've allowed for it to disappear into the deepest realms of our minds. The Black Panther movement of the 1960's is well known, though it's usually taught in a misrepresenting light. They only sought for the equality of our people, decent schools for our children and a non dictatorial roll of the police departments. The U.S. government (with the aid of an infiltrator) killed or incarcerated the leaders on a variety of false charges. I will not fail to mention the internal disputes too played a role in their destruction.

However, the fact remains, people can be killed or arrested, but ideas whose time has come is unstoppable. It doesn't matter what strength the opposition has. The greatest thing in the world isn't where we stand, but what direction we're moving in. Have we reasonably considered the direction that we're moving in as a whole? Our desire for consciousness will increase our receptivity of it not the increase of wealth, because those who are willing to sacrifice the quest for wealth are a wonderful thing to have in our quest for awareness. And those whose main goal is for riches, they deserve neither riches nor liberty.

There is a trend among our people of "keeping it real," but that has a capacity of keeping us down. Our people need to hear what they need to know, not what they want to hear. We are warriors by birth, and the Art of War is simple; "find out where your enemy is and get at him as soon as possible to strike at him as hard as you can and keep moving." Ulysses S. Grant borrowing from Sun Tzu. Unfortunately, we've accepted a false notion that our brothers from another section of town, or some other minor difference, relegates them to enemy status. In the reception of that type of thinking lies an enemy rooting for the destruction of us as a whole.

To be successful, a soldier must know how man reacts. Man hasn't really changed, despite the sophistication of the weapons in his arsenal and their capacity to annihilate all life forms on this earth. We need to realize that the enemy of our brother is our enemy as well, yet till we realize that gang affiliations or, these other type of differences are ceased, we'll continue to be perpetrators of genocide. This is nothing less than a strategic tactic used against us and as long as we focus on each other in a negative light, we'll never focus on the adversarial society which targets us for destruction. When oppressive men combine to enact oppressive measures, we must unify or fall one by one, as an unpitied sacrifice in a futile struggle.

We have to be willing to fight in order to overcome unconsciousness, because it is not easily defeated. It must also be noted that consciousness without action is just as bad as unconsciousness with the wrong action. The fact that we are aware of something does no good if we're not acting in the best interest of that knowledge or information. It is one thing to reveal to a man his mistakes, but it's another thing to show him the correct way. I know that in order to unify a large group of people will be a difficult task, but I also know to continue to allow ourselves to be divided is to cause for our strength to dissipate. That is easy when people are unconscious to the manipulative tactics of this society.

We've been born in a society that teaches and molds our thinking to believe that we're 3rd or 4th class citizens. This country has shown this so clearly so often, however the debacle of the 2005 hurricane Katrina brought this to a more visible level than many would have cared to admit. New Orleans, pre-Katrina, was city of over half a million inhabitants nearly 50% of those were "African American." The world was shocked at the images of a city virtually under water; estimates calculated 80% under water.

Thousands of residents were on the rooftops of houses and more were crammed into the sports "Super Dome." The "help us" signs were of no real consequence. The American government waited four days before dispatching aid even though multiple media helicopters arrived in New Orleans to report the worst natural disaster in recent history, the American government still sat idly by. I have no doubt that had it hit any area where it's prominent members of society (Caucasians primarily), the government would have been in full gear in such a prompt reaction so as to defy physics.

This brought another sobering reality to the fore front; we can be left to die because we were dependant on someone else to come "rescue" us. Obviously, the government had an obligation to assist its citizens, but evidently when you're a 3rd or 4th class citizen, you really can expect aid on their time. I do know the poverty issue was pertinent to the fiasco, but the poverty is entangled with "race" so often that it's almost inter-changeable. Many African Americans are blessed with an abundance of wealth but so many of the less fortunate are forgotten.

Not only did the Bush junior administration wait four days before it decided to send aid, it brought in Caucasian contractors in for the purpose of "rebuilding," despite the fact that closer to the destruction was an African American contractor attempting to get the government contract, it was a no bid contract. This means that simply put, the administration just gave it to who the president wanted to have it. According to the Associated Press, only 1.5% of the FEMA contracts were given to African Americans disregarding the 5% standard established by the government.

It's further shown by the fact that the tourist attracting sector, *French Quarter was quickly rebuilt, along with the "Super Dome," though that may have possibly have been with private money. The remainder of the city was left up to the benevolence of volunteers, who are responsible for the vast majority of the progress that has been made. To further show our value, a Native African was murdered moments after; the hurricane only showed their actions how we are used to seeing them. It didn't matter that the murdered victim was cuffed.

Their acquittal goes into a long list of exonerated assassins wearing badges. In 2005 the Department Of Justice reported that 136 deaths by the hands of police were all deemed justified and that African Americans are twelve times more likely to be sent to prison. With statistics like that, it's amazing that not many of us are willing to stop being complacent in ignorance and seek illumination from the lies.

This type of police behavior exists in all 50 states in this country, yet people won't realize that it won't stop while most of us are unconscious, rather callous to its existence. We must raise our conscious and stop behaving as if we have no conscience. Considering nearly 2000 died from Katrina because of a reliance on the government, but in their defense, it was the government's position to assist them. We can't expect someone to help us if it's merely a "job," but not their desire to do so.

This is the same government which lied about freeing slaves if they fought for them in the Revolutionary War. This is also the same government which lied about freed slaves receiving forty acres and a mule. This is the same government which killed and imprisoned the Black Panther Party leadership simply because they attempted to fight against social injustices against African Americans. This is the same government, only names have changed. I don't mean to imply some things haven't gotten better, but on a large scale, it seems that things remain the same.

We have thousands of African American millionaires and dozens of African American billionaires, yet I don't wish for anyone to believe that I'm proposing for them to relinquish their wealth, but I do propose at least a 1% donation to a common cause in order to ensure that the next time we need help, we aren't sitting on top of the roof with corpses floating around us waiting on the government. Surely, 1% could be spared for such a fund to help impoverished communities. Many of them spend more than that on jewelry and or cars.

Even with monetary investments, it will require more people only give a little when we give only money, but when we give of ourselves, we then truly distribute wealth. I'm not naive enough to think all native Africans will be willing to give up 1% to help with the survival of our posterity, even though they have no problem giving to the same government which largely causes for us to fend for ourselves. If we believe that we can't achieve something, then as long as no one attempts at it, assuredly we won't. We all can agree that this society will NEVER advocate our unif-ication or for our consciousness to be raised. It has too much to lose if we become either.

The idea of us helping fund our own assistance may seem like a lot of things to a lot of different people, even within our own communities, but its main function is to have readily available aid for our less fortunate in preparation for the next man made or natural disaster. I'm not implying that we have a virtual "piggy bank" for the less fortunate at the wealthy's expense, but for us collectively to be helpful, not just vocally indignant at the government for their lack of concern for people when a disaster strikes. It's naive to believe that a society that continually berates, ignores, vilifies and incarcerate us on a systematic basis, to be willing to help us in our time of need.

We can't expect for them to be our "knight in shining armor" because the only armor we could expect to see is the riot gear they so willingly put on anytime more than a handful of brothers are together voicing their dissent at any of the multiple problems which afflict us. Obviously, a lot of planning and careful observation would have to be put in place, but there is nothing that dedicated and sincere African Americans can't achieve when focused. We owe it to our future generation to at least try.

The usefulness of wealth is better than merely possessing it; we can't let our possessions possess us. The more we love ourselves collectively, the less of ourselves individually will we think about. No matter what field we're in, our success is always based on the sacrifices of others. There aren't many of us so inwardly strong that we aren't influenced by external circumstances. These outward circumstances are either motivational or they're discouragements, but they are probably responsible in our becoming what we became: good or bad.

We may never have had Tupac had his mother never been a drug addict; we may never have had a Malcolm X had he never went to prison or we may have never had a Nat Turner had he not been born into slavery. Adversity reveals the character of the person whose dealing with it and it requires that we deal with it promptly. We may always have adversity, but to be conscious about what we're dealing with and how we are to deal with them makes all the difference between overcoming adversity or it overcoming us.

I'm confident in the strength of our people to effectively deal with the issues which afflict us, whether it be genocide, gang violence or drug devastation, but I'm just as confident in the fact that as long as we lack unity and communications between our extraordinary and ordinary, we'll always have a divide and as long as this separation exists due to the propagation of society, we'll have one class of our people behaving as if the less fortunate of our heritage mean little.

And on the other side to that will be the less fortunate will resent the privileged and regard them suspiciously because it behooves them how they have at their disposal means to help alleviate the suffering of their community, yet refuse to. I don't intend to present money as a "cure all," because we see some of the wealthiest people on earth (regardless of heritage) behaving foolishly, but it could be a huge aid in the lives of some of our less fortunate, this not just on an economic plane, but on a psychological plane. They can know that those who've made it out of those same situations have not forgotten those who still have the misfortune to be still in them.

It has been said that a "poverty of purpose is far worse than a poverty of purse." It's beyond dispute that native Africans have so much excellence without conscious or conscience, but can you imagine if they obtained both of them? We've seen the social "elitists" in our heritage, but in such behavior they simply are allowing for themselves to be morally bankrupt, and in regards to our heritage-disloyal. How can we thrive when we belittle consciousness, education, and achievement? How could we thrive glorifying wealth and ignorance?

This isn't the proper preservation that our posterity need nor should we be interested in it. Our unconsciousness has become our greatest liability because it causes for attention to be placed on so many non-healthy false concepts of liberty. And these are the things that have been advertised as the things we should seek to obtain. We need to dedicate ourselves to reclaiming the excellence that our ancestry possessed. If not, our communities will continue to be destroyed from within and from without. We have enough external negative influences and devices that threaten to destroy us from without.

It baffles me that the American government can consistently claim that each war they've taken to a foreign land is based on a premise of bringing "democracy" and "freedom," but the Native African communities have not really benefitted from those laudable ideals. I don't mean to imply that they never involve themselves where tyranny is prevalent, but they need to be true practitioners of it in their own country to its citizens; ALL of its citizens.

Many are vague in their recollection of the Rwandan massacre of 1994. This was one of the worst genocides in recent history perpetrated under Bill Clinton's administration. The Hutu clan murdered close to a million Tutsi clan members, with no intervention from the U.S. government. The African Americans still consider him their favorite president (next to Barack Obama) despite he found it so easy to casually disregard the lives of the slaughtered Africans, not to mention his "3 strikes" law.

It is indisputable that many people prospered monetarily during his presidency, but that alone does not outweigh his blatant disregard for people of African lineage. That misguided law is still devastating the African American communities. Tragically we see misguided loyalty shown by our communities, but this stems from an ignorance of what his "left hand was doing." WE were too busy looking at the perceived "gifts" in his right hand. We should stop being so enamored at perceived gifts, but to realize what spirit it was given in. We have to learn to stop expecting "gifts" from people and to realize that if we did receive something from someone, it's merely a loan; we will pay for it.

The ramifications of his presidency still resonate with us today. Thousands of people have been "lost" to the system for virtually nothing. Definitely nothing worth losing their freedom forever warrants. It's sad because we were already disproportionately sent to prison before that, but now that just compounded an already dire situation. I don't seek to justify criminal behavior but truly a life sentence for the theft of some food or some other frivolous act is disturbing. It should disturb every citizen in this country which prides itself on being a "fair and just nation."

All too often our people only see what they wish to see, we can't allow for any ones past seemingly good deeds to excuse them from responsibility for present devastating acts. They can still be deemed present because our communities have lost a whole generation to those unjust laws. According to the J.S. Sentencing Committee, we consist of 50% of the incarcerated for cocaine, but also according to them Hispanics and Caucasians use of this drug is 70%. So, obviously Bill didn't need to throw the brothers away with his "3 strikes law," we were already being decimated by the courts.

We can be wiser if we learned from our fore fathers from Africa that, by and large, this government has not changed drastically enough for us to allow for illusions to be considered as reality. What we depend on is mostly dependant of what we've learned. All that we need to do is pay attention to the past and it will show us everything we need to know. If we refuse to battle for ourselves when we could possibly win without violence or if we won't battle when our victory isn't too costly, we may find ourselves at a place when we will have to battle when all odds are against us and we only have a slight chance of survival.

We may even find ourselves in a worst position; fighting when there's no chance of victory. It is better to die free than to live in bondage, yet we're mostly responsible for our bondage due to our unconsciousness which fuels our destiny. If we refuse to establish a link between ourselves when times don't call for it, in times that they WILL call for it, we most likely won't heed that call either. We must be willing to reach out to each other or we will continue to diminish our capabilities as a people. It is time that we open our eyes to consciousness to stop the current blinded vision we suffer from.

CHAPTER 3
Who Do We Believe In?

We native Africans, as a whole, may very well be the most religious people on earth. We definitely are in the top three. You could view that statement as a positive or negative, but it can't really be denied. We have strong beliefs that had it not been for the grace of God, we very well may have been exterminated like the ancient Aztecs. I must emphasis they do have a lineage still in existence today, though in the form of the Native Americans.

God's intervention on the behalf of the African people prevented the wholesale slaughter of the African people. The transatlantic slave trade took slavery to an entire different plane than the slavery Africans had suffered at the hands of other Africans, not even the slavery we endured at the hands of the Arabians or the Spanish compared. Many may not have known that they owned African slaves before the Americas did, but the Arabians, Spaniards owned their own people as slaves as well and didn't necessarily consider themselves as superior to the slaves they owned, ethnically speaking.

The connection we feel towards God for delivering us is akin to the way the Israelites felt at God for delivering them from the Egyptian pharaoh.

And just like the Israelites, we too have seemingly forgotten this; this is what our behavior suggests. Africans born in America have two main belief structures: Christianity and Islam. We have few Catholics and Jehovah's Witnesses, but the previous afore mentioned make up the majority of our belief system. Yet, even in those 2 we have several different "denominations." Within Islam we have the Sunni, Shiite, five percent of the Nation of Islam, which is the more prominent in America.

We seem content with enclosing ourselves into our own "denomination" at the expense of a unity of those who may not view things identically. It's as if we no longer believe that our spirituality and community service is connected and crucial to the lives of our posterity. If we had more people realizing this, our communities would be in much better positions. We need understanding of each other's view because this will lead to more meaningful conversations and communication between people of different faiths. This could have the potential to show our youth who have different gang affiliations that no matter how our opinions may vary, we can still be unified on a common goal which should be for the elevation of their consciousness.

There is another hoped for goal, it is that we honor God and not simply ideals we grasp on to. People of different faiths may differ in ideas, but there is no basis for hating someone with a different point of view. The Bible says, "What I say to you who are listening, continue to love your enemies, to do good to those who hate you and your reward will be great, and you will be the sons of the most HIGH, because he is kind toward the unthankful and wicked." (Luke 6 v. 27, 35)

The Qur'an states a similar concept. In Surah 60: 7, it states "it may be that Allah will bring about friendship between you and those of them whom you hold as enemies. And Allah is powerful, forgiving and merciful." The saying in reality is that we seem to "have just enough religion to hate, but not enough to love each other." This was a wise recognition of Jonathon Swift. Love is the one trait that everybody preaches, but few practice it. It seems that the entire world is content to hearing love being spoken, but not practiced.

Nowhere as much, so it seems, as our community's descent from royalty, then enslaved in misery only presently to reside in unconsciousness. True consciousness forces us to realize that we are made in God's image, thinking realistically, we fail to even walk in His shadow. We could rightfully argue that we've endured more assaults on our identity than any other group of people. Our fractured and misguided identity caused by social injustices still doesn't justify our continued acceptance of un-consciousness and ignorance, though those two are virtually inter-changeable.

We need to be concerned with our legacy and what types of foundations we're leaving for our future generations. Our foundations should be based on progress and in our progress, we must destroy the things which seek to destroy us: drug dependency, celebration of criminality, misogyny and genocide, just to name a few things which CONSISTENTLY present themselves before us in problematic levels. The fact simply is that our youth commit all of these types of acts because it is their learned behavior. They learned it from the adults.

We can't depend on this society to help us re-define our youth; we can't count on anyone to fall down to help us up. I know our spiritual agenda sometimes seem to conflict with our social agenda, but they're both in need of addressing. No man with faith IN God hasn't at least once questioned God and asked how come it seems that we're continually oppressed, yet few ask themselves what they can do about the oppression they see. Some are tempted to just "let go and let God," but God will not move when men fail to move.

The ramifications of our unconsciousness have our men killing themselves off in unprecedented rates in this country, not to mention in many parts of Africa. Speaking of African genocide, the Bush Jr. administration adopted the same policy that Clinton's did in regard to the Rwandan genocide. The genocide in Darfur is being allowed to continue even after several years of bloodshed. It goes to show that when African people are the victims of atrocities, the U.S. government never finds any reason to intervene.

So it doesn't matter which political party is in office, our value to them is shown to be of little.

This present massacre has a death toll exceeding a million as well and had been going on for at least of the Bush Jr. administration, about 5 years. With thoughts of Rwanda, Darfur and "Katrina," we can see a pattern of consistent neglect of African people by the U.S. government. This same government which invaded Iraq twice, Afghanistan and many other "Middle Eastern" countries on the premise of bringing them "democracy," even though they didn't ask for the U.S. governments help. There is nothing so strong as the truth, yet it is often disbelieved.

We can't let our faith in God and ourselves to be diminished because of a trust in a government which has failed us more times than anyone could remember. These institutions fail us so often that it baffles me that we allow for ourselves to EVER believe in them again. We have long had a responsibility to God, our family, our communities and ourselves. For some strange reason however, for the past couple decades we've placed ourselves first, then our communities (friends, associates) second, our family (if them) thirdly and lastly God. Yet, the last two have been virtually ignored by many.

This is partly (mostly) because of the modern societies who have brainwashed us into falling victim to materialism, not to mention unconsciousness, and that we should seek our pleasure before anything else. It tells us that we need to live for the "now" and in that, the richer a man is, the more he is held to be. This is sadly the rationale of many, and this thinking has crept into the ideals of many churches. They fail to realize that when God is on our side that we are in the majority, regardless to the numerous enemies we have against us, not to mention ourselves.

We must realize that when we fail to act in the best interest of our families and communities, we are operating outside of God's plans for us. Our spiritual position doesn't negate our African heritage, nor does it negate our responsibility to our community, as stated before. We can't be foolish enough to believe our heritage disappeared because of our belief in God being the creator of ALL men.

In this society we've been fed images of strength and power and most of our earlier identifications are from perceptions of how strong we are in the physical or how much we possess monetarily. It's not shocking that most of our males measure their worth by those false standards. Education is not viewed as importantly as it needs to, though this education system is far from 100% accurate, it definitely is a catalyst for further, more correct learning. In many states African Americans graduate high School less than 50% as opposed to more than 70% of Caucasian students according to the Justice Policy Institute report of 2006.

It is worth re-iterating that the education system rooted in the American society is not one which could be equated with the thought of helping Native Africans consciousness, the vast majority of material in their schools are inept at consciously educating its children, educational faults of this system should not be used as an excuse to not educate oneself.

42

Those who use this as an excuse are willingly giving themselves over to unconsciousness; this means that they aren't any better than those who are unwillingly unconscious.

They base their ideas on a flawed idea that since they did not know, they are less responsible, but ignorance can't be excused when one had the opportunity at acquiring some form of knowledge. Minds have been compared to parachutes, only functioning correctly when their opened, but so often we have become accustomed at keeping them closed; closed minds, caused by prejudices against anyone who believes differently than we do. People aren't willing to let people believe what they choose to, though they themselves enjoy that privilege.

Naturally our thoughts and tolerance will grow in increments, but we let them spread so minutely that we're satisfied with keeping ourselves inside of our separated belief systems at the expense of getting close to our brother. This type of behavior is anti spiritual. It's also divisive. We seem to disbelieve that in our efforts to help others, we help ourselves. The devastation and divisions man has caused under the guise of "religion" is well documented: Darfur; the Spanish inquisition; September 11th and the Crusades just to name a few. More have died in the name of God than for any other reason, and very few have been just.

Men have a sacrificial nature when it comes to God, but when it's misguided; the potential for damage is greater than almost anything imaginable. Men who are at odds for political reasons can come to agreements much quicker than when men feel they're in possession of God behind their cause. Men never do evil so completely and cheerfully as when they perpetrate it from a religious stand point. Life is short enough without us killing each other for religious differences.

If we could, learn (would' learn) to channel our energies in a more positive behavior, we would see a drastic change in our communities. I'm aware that we don't make up a large number of "suicide bombers," but the divisions and disdain found in Muslims and Christian's heart toward each other is heart breaking. He who knows only his side of a cause knows only a little. The same can be said of one's faith. My desire is for our unity; it will seem impossible to some, but those are the ones who aren't willing to help bring it to pass; or those who don't wish for it to be obtained.

I'm aware that a lot of work will be needed in order to make even the slightest advancement, but it is well worth the risk. The majority of us will never be content with society, but until we've realized that this society hasn't treated us equally nor should we.

We must realize that until all of us are free, none of us truly are. So, evidently unity is needed. We will never be unified until we come to a greater level of consciousness; what advantages consciousness entails. Awareness of who the enemy is crucial to us, just as awareness of who we are is crucial to our posterity. Everyone who comes to us with smothering kindness and rhetoric claiming to be assisting us doesn't automatically mean they're telling the truth. This U.S. government has done that to us a number of times.

We should realize that though our spiritual beliefs may be different in the Native African community, we are still striving for a common goal; a closeness to God. Obviously, we have various expressions, but that should not cause us to be untrusting of our brothers. A difference in our ideals about God worship, this should not cause us to fail to focus on the larger tasks at hand; unification of our communities, happily aiding with the raising of our youths' consciousness. Sadly, many of our adults are unconscious themselves, but are unaware and those unaware of that will suffer the greatest disadvantage in this society, it's usually us.

There exists inside of us what we need to bring to pass our deliverance, but many still find themselves loyal to a society which they erroneously believe will rid itself of its ingrained prejudices and hypocrisy. These underlying basic foundations of this country will not be easily rectified. Despite my assertion that the U.S. Constitution should be for us, I'm conscious that it was made EXCLUSIVELY for its Caucasian citizens. Wisely stated by the Minister Louis Farrakhan, "Native Americans, Blacks (Native Africans), and all other non-whites were to be the burden bearers of this country."

So it should be no strange happening that we can't seem to reap the benefits of it standing, rather applying to us. This is why it had been ratified to distance itself from the original position that "blacks" were' only three fifths of a man. So, our identity crisis is rooted in the reality that on every turn we have proof of a system that was not established with our best interest, rather none of our interest, in mind. A reason our oppression still exists is that we, as a whole unit, lack consciousness of what it is that they need to do. Our modern religious leaders are failing the community. They, along with our so- called political leaders, ought to be working in a manner conducive to the advancement of our people, not to advance their political agendas or ideas on how to create more personal wealth for themselves.

It's a tragedy to see political and religions content with seeing so much poverty in areas of our communities with another community demonstrating such wealth.

Until we're discontented with mediocrity, which is even prevalent in people respective faiths, until we're willing to help the less fortunate in our communities raise themselves and their consciousness from this abstract freedom that they (we) possess, we'll continue to see things existing as they currently are. As with all things abstract, it really doesn't exist. Abraham Lincoln said, "Our progress in degeneracy appears to be pretty rapid as a nation, we began by declaring all men are created equal. We now practically read, all men are created equal, except the Negroes, foreigners and Catholics. When it comes to this, I shall prefer immigrating to some country where they make no pretense of loving liberty-to Russia for instance, where despotism can be taken pure and without the base alloy of hypocrisy."

Such an insightful statement from the man celebrated for his supposed "Emancipation Of Proclamation." Those who wish to deprive us of liberty don't deserve it themselves. I KNOW that God is just, so they won't be able to keep it because of their hypocrisy. No man who is willing to exploit another cannot expect for their exploitation to not soon come. It's sad that some of our own religious leaders exploit us with the idea that God will intervene on our behalf, even when we fail to move. We can't seek to expect for Him to make it easy and to strengthen us to overcome while we aid in the destruction of ourselves. I suppose they aren't familiar with scripture which states that "Faith without works is dead." (James 2v. 25)

I don't doubt God's ability and willingness to assist us, because He's done so throughout history, but I don't believe He will move on behalf of our communities if we don't move on our own behalf. It is evident many spiritual leaders have unfamiliar concepts with the ministry of Christ: He fed the hungry, healed the sick and accepted the outcasts of His society. (Mark 8 v. 1-10, Matthew 8 v. 16, John 4 v. 5-42) These are not isolated incidents of Christ showing kindness and healing for His social surroundings, but only examples of His character, which His followers are to mimic.

It seems far too often that we mimic the traits of His persecutors because He wasn't into the way of things being done as they done them: religiously. We cannot worry about the outcome before we even begin. We must set the foundations, even if we're unable to see the full fruition of our plans. We can be comforted knowing that we're raising warriors up to take our place in the fight for our people. It is irrelevant how insignificant our start may seem because once we begin, it's destined to end.

There's no luck or chance involved, because foolish men believe in luck, but wise man believe in work and persevering. We can't continue to sit by watching our communities further destroy themselves because of our familial principles are devastated in a major way. Forty three percent of our women are raising their children on their own, compared to just 13% of Caucasian women in this country. This is according to the U.S. Census Bureau. Our men generally pay more attention to their cars instead of their children. How can our children excel when this society expects the worst from them, their schools expect the least from them and men in their own communities think nothing of them?

If we don't repair our family unit, we'll continue to see self destructive behavior from our communities threatening our children's future. We can't afford to keep allowing divisions in our communities. We must stop allowing for religious, or class or any other difference to separate us further. We must exemplify a Love from God, which will show us unifying with others and lifting others up who are consciously or unconsciously, destroying our communities.

I'm aware of the fact that many of our people don't necessarily heed' to the teachings of Christ or Islam, but to believe in God means to live as if

He exists, yearning to be in his presence, but this will never be done if we don't love our brother. It is almost irrelevant what we believe in individually, but we must all agree that our communities and our posterity MUST be a priority. Minister Louis Farrakhan is a prime example of one who has made it his life's mission to attempt to raise the consciousness of the African American. The Million Man March in 1995 and the Millions More Movement in 2005 are 2 examples of his relentless attempts at unifying people of African ancestry, despite the multitude of differences we have.

Sadly, many of even our own people misconstrue his efforts at unifying us as if this means that we are to be prejudiced against other ethnic groups. Our unification isn't indicative of a need to be "anti" anyone. This media, however, has a LARGE SWAY OVER OUR PEOPLE, this makes no sense.

According to Dorfman, L. and Schiraldi, V 2001 b "Off Balance: Youth, Race, and Crime in the news, Full Report." this study show African Americans and Hispanics overrepresented as perpetrators in news reports, especially violent crimes, and underrepresented as victims. This merely shows how biased the media coverage we receive is tilted towards a negative light regarding us. The unconscious Native African believes that this same media is some type of unbiased reporting institution; which is a far cry from the truth.

They also have the mistaken notion that anyone who speaks against oppressive and prejudice government is guilty of "anti-Americanism" and are trying to cause some type of "race war" or revolution. The thing about a revolution is one either wins or dies. We need to be willing to accept whatever of those options we must. .Any one should know that just because violence may have been used to gain liberty from tyrants, this doesn't mean that violence won't have to be used again in the future.

Some of our peoples' minds have been so distorted with this western ideology that it equates the media's reports as some type of "'gospel Truth." The unconscious mind is unsure of what it wants; it sees of the continued atrocities committed against us, but still puts faith in the social structure which perpetuates them on a constant basis. The beginning of seeking consciousness is difficult, but those who seek it must be prepared to be confronted at every turn. Nothing ought to be greater to our people than our collective consciousness. And nothing is so hard that it can't be solved by perseverance.

We must be determined to defeat, at all costs, in spite of all obstacles, no matter how much time and how difficult the road will be, unconsciousness. If we don't prepare our self to be victorious, then we are preparing for defeat. We can't depend on anyone else's nobility to ensure our security and survival. If we value anything more than our liberty and equality, then I feel we deserve neither. We will continue to lose both of them. It's ironic that if we find comfort or money as more of a priority, we will willingly forfeit our people's liberty and equality for it. If we don't think about our children's future, the future they can expect obviously will be similar to the present; hopeless.

This preoccupation with wealth has been damaging on two fronts: the wealth that has been obtained by some of us causes for them to seek acceptance from this western society. It has been shown through the trials of O. J. Simpson and Michael Jackson (just to name a few), that no matter what amount of success they may have achieved, they're still only third or fourth class citizens once a criminal accusation has been made. The odd thing is that all were acquitted in a "court of law," but once the charge has been made, for all intents and purposes, they're guilty.

The civil suits against Kobe and O. J. brought about a verdict others wanted, and once Michael was acquitted, the I.R.S. suddenly was interested in his finances. The point is obvious; when the system sets its sights on you and you're an African American, you can rest assure, it will get you, in one way or another.

Another example of hypocrisy by this western media is it's vilification of NFL star Michael Vick. He pled guilty to funding dog fights and gambling. I don't condone the abuse of animals, but I do wish to bring to light the fact the media shows and the outrage with their reporting of this ordeal. It seems that it's irrelevant that the police tend to kill 100's of its native African citizens, all without any real public disapproval. In 2005 alone, we had over 134 instances where the police killed native African citizens; this doesn't even take into consideration the number of Caucasian or other ethnicities they are allowed to murder.

We are being removed from the face of the earth by government officials, yet it seems acceptable; this, because of the western mindset that we're expendable anyway. We had less coverage of ex-vice president Cheney shooting someone in the face than we had at Michael Vicks lapse of judgment. How often can we look into the history books and say we had a vice president of this country shoot someone in the face? That alone should have warranted more coverage than a football player's "animal cruelty." This just goes to show at how mercilessly we're sought after for any real, or imagined, crime.

It is a devastating ordeal to be caught up in the legal system if you don't have the means to pay some lawyer to increase the odds of your receiving a more "fair" trial. They are by no means a guarantee that you'll be given all the rights afforded to you, but it does weigh the scales of "justice" a little more in your favor.

Another recent example of the blatant and frequent racism shown in our society is the Native African group of teenagers termed the "Jena 6" with the blatant display of racism one could easily mistake himself as being in the 1950s instead of being in 2005.

To those who may have been under a rock when this occurred, the following is a summary of it: a group of Native African teenagers sat under a tree designated for the Caucasian students at their Louisiana high school. The next day, some Caucasian students hung three nooses from the tree. Those students received two days suspension for what the school faculty deemed "a childish prank."

For anybody who grew up in America, the symbolization of a noose invokes a multitude of ideas, but being deemed "a childish prank" is nowhere in that concept. All Africans in this country know that when a noose is hung by ESPECIALLY Caucasians, it's nothing comical about it. It's threatening to say the least.

The racism goes deeper though; some Caucasian students beat up one of the African American students at the school and busted his head with a bottle. They received probation from the town's district attorney. About a week later, the brother who had his head busted and allegedly, with 5 others beat up a Caucasian student who may or may not have been involved with his assault. The Caucasian student was released from the hospital within 3 hours, but the "Jena 6" were charged with attempted murder despite NO eyewitnesses, they were ultimately convicted, and facing 25 years in jail behind that. It didn't matter that all 5 were between 15-17 years old.

It's not surprising that of the 3000 people in the town, only 300 or so are "African 'American" obviously, an all Caucasian jury wouldn't dream of acquitting some "black boy" for assaulting their precious children. I have no doubt that if the majority of the jury had it their way, they would have taken the nooses the Caucasian students had, hung them on the tree and lynched the "Jena 6" themselves and then called it a day. Fortunately, the publicity on this town has caused for them to somewhat revise their way of dealing with this. I must clarify, only one was convicted at the time of this writing and Michael Bell was given a new trial and it was sent to juvenile court, where it belonged at first. Others had their charges dropped and others pled to lesser offenses, but had the media not caught wind of this, all six of them would quite probably be doing 25 years in prison.

It was clearly the media which swayed the events to turn around, because the Louisiana prosecutor implicitly stated that "they will be prosecuted to the furthest extent of the law." No one of our heritage ever really doubted that anyway, but for him to say it outright takes it to another place. Whether they say it or not, this country's prosecutors behave in that fashion anyway. As stated earlier the Bureau of Justice reporting we compromise of over 60% of individuals in jail, but only 12.9% of the country's population. (Report issued June 30, 2007)

I don't wish to seem like I justify violence committed by anybody against anybody, but I MOST DEFINITELY don't condone a double standard in this "justice" system. It just goes on to continue to perpetuate the idea that our lives are worth less than any and everybody else's. The fact that this story grabbed at the country was simply because it was publicized and had it not been the "Jena 6" would have found themselves a part of the staggering statistics. I suppose that since things turned out not as bad as they could have, the "African American" community believes that all is right in this world. They can't be further from the truth.

I hate to appear as some type of cynic, but we see unfair practices in the law committed against us in the most liberal states, as well as the most conservative states; in fact, if it's one thing only the Republicans and Democrats can agree on, it's that they only utilize us for furtherance of their career, and once in office, its back to ignoring the issues which affect us, or cause more archaic legislation designed to further decimate our community. I don't imply heartfelt concern for our people isn't felt by anyone in either of those respective parties, but they definitely are in the minority (numerically speaking).

At least the Republican Party makes no illusions about who their primary focus is on - the rich. They know we know how they feel about us, so no deviation from their ideals is shown, so when they push for the agendas which benefit their core group, it's no surprise.

However, the Democratic Party has had our loyalty for far too long and we still receive mere "crumbs" from the table and we have to fight for those. Our people who have the good fortune to gain enough wealth shouldn't allow for that to over shadow the necessity of our communities to gain a consciousness of what EXACTLY we are dealing with in this society, and be willing to aid when possible.

Many of the conscious minded are tired of seeing our people being taught that we have no place, or at least we only have a limited purpose in this society, mainly relegating us to the entertainment fields or sports. Thoughts like these continually wreak havoc in our communities, not to mention confusion. This prevents us from reaching or maximizing our potential capability in this society. We can't allow for such fictitious ideas to keep being perpetuated. It suppresses our goals and depresses our people because we're oppressed by this society's ideas about what we should be and do.

The innate warrior nature that we possess has constantly been misunderstood by society, labeling us violent or belligerent. Sadly, we've misappropriated our GOD given strength and by preying on our own communities. We need clear eyes on who we need to be, typically, we all are desirous of justice, but the concept has been so elusive for us to obtain that we've basically given up on the search for it. It's a well established fact that the rich rob from the poor, but far too often the poor in our communities rob from each other. This is done because this is the way society has taught them (us) to behave.

To see justice, we will first have to recognize consciousness and morality because without that caring from our communities, we will continue to see our people mislead by false ideals about what society says we are. The irony is that this nation so often feigns to be ignorant of the injustices it's delivering to its own citizens. This has the capacity for a nation to be diminished in its position. We've already witnessed a majority of the world call America on its hypocrisy, with regards to its "minority" citizens. Most Americans attempt to relegate any criticism of this land as mere jealousy, and some of the countries may very well be envious of this country, but several are in better economic positions than this country and they treat their citizens better than this country. Canada, Belgium and Switzerland just to name a few, yet they're quite vocal on the treatment America affords its "minority" citizens.

The world is tired of this country imposing its will on smaller countries under the premise of democracy while its own citizens are being denied it on American soil. As long as inequality resides as the normal for people of African descent, liberty will never reside for the American people as a whole. Their desire to save humanity is usually always a facade to rule it.

William Shirer once said, "America may be the first country in which fascism takes power through democratic election." How evident this seems to be to the rest of the world. We've overcome some atrocities that would have eradicated us a long time ago had we not been inherently prepared to withstand them. But our physical ability to withstand will not be sufficient to guarantee our children's survival. We must at least take them to a place where they can have a chance for survival. We must give them a chance for success, without society sabotaging them. We have to de-program them and ourselves to stop accepting the opinions of this western society and stop allowing for ourselves to sub-consciously judge each other based on the standards of this society.

We've even allowed for our faith to be misleading us into believing that Yeshua ("Jesus") looks like some type of Caucasian model. The fact that people always say it doesn't matter what color he is, and I agree it doesn't, but I will not allow for the Caucasians to claim another central figure in history as theirs if he wasn't. The fact that he was born in the "Middle East" seems to be of no concern to them, I could suppose that's because they've been so successful at guiding other's perceptions for so long, their confidence is in that ability to tell us the "piss on our leg" is merely rain. Sadly, we're willing to believe the lies, despite the obvious stench.

One of the greatest things we could know is our self and in the knowing of our true self, the enemy will reveal himself swiftly and oppose our efforts vehemently. We must be willing to get to a conscious state where our next generation means more to us than our own lives. We cannot afford to doubt our cause; doubt is the greatest enemy to a man's cause or faith. It will never assist us in things which would benefit us; instead, it whispers to us that all of our efforts are futile. I hope I could speak for the masses who believe as I do that our efforts and our death (if needed) won't be in vain.

Our attempts to make a better future for our children will have a difficult start, but anything worthwhile will. I can think of nothing more worthy than our posterity. We have no choice but to make a successful end of the endeavor. It can be done if we strive and persevere to together. I believe that the value of an idea is the amount of sacrifice we're willing to put into it to bring it to fruition. Obviously there will be differences of opinions, but the primary goal is accomplishing the task of combining our efforts so that no one person should seek to obtain all the credit for a task which will clearly take the collective efforts of all of us. We all are suffering because of the disunity and unconsciousness which afflicts our community.

So in essence, those who desire for us to be unified must be willing to fulfill their function, whatever it maybe. We must do it in spite of whatever personal repercussion, if Nat Turner could suffer death for what he believed in (our peoples' freedom) then surely we could suffer potential monetary loss or slander.

So many of our people are wounded from within and are unsure of how to find the healing from such injury. So, the answers are sought after through all types of self gratifying sources. Many are carrying the weight of childhood abuse and' its residual affects remain, only to be compounded by the abuse society leaves them with; low self esteem and unhealthy images of themselves. Plus, we have so few fathers involved with their children, whether through neglect on their part or the fact that many African American women use their children as leverage against the fathers by not allowing for the father to see them.

It's without doubt that many of our people are in need of consciousness; a consciousness that their "domestic war" yields only children as the casualty, many times causing hostility towards one or both parents. If we realize that we're products of our history, then it is necessary for us to know our future is dependent on the history we make today. When we raise bitter children that will usually cause for them to be bitter adults and further perpetuate what has been done to them, instead of concerning themselves with how to make sure they don't allow for themselves to continue the cycle in their children.

These are some of the types we have in our churches; so willing to receive God's forgiveness and unwilling to demonstrate it towards others. It's easy to forget how our spiritual beliefs are as important to our consciousness (social) as ignorance is to our unconsciousness. The consciousness (spirituality) gives us an illumination of our mental capabilities, because aware minds are more prepared minds and we are under a responsibility to try and alleviate the suffering so dominant in our communities. It's sad that many have disregarded the full extent of our suffering in this society, even in our religious practitioners.

Our love for ourselves ought to be so strong that it captures us and helps us determine the best route for our youth. Without us facilitating consciousness in our children, they will never have the liberty beyond the present abstract liberty we now possess. The pride of people to aid in encouraging our youth elevate them, plus this reward will be priceless. We should all seek it. We must be aware that there is nothing as painful as being in bondage (mental OR physical), and no bondage is as painful as that of unconsciousness.

We must strive to teach our children things worth learning, while they learn how to forget things not worth knowing, which is a majority of

American History. With each truth they've taught they've inter-mingled it with falsehoods; with each year that has passed, more credence is given to their lies. The confusion this wreaks in our minds is almost irreparable. The longer we've been taught some specific fact or habit, the more difficult it is to remove our self from it. A conscious mind can look so directly, in tensely, so penetratingly that it can see through the "his-story" experience propagates and see it for what it really is. We will either be corrupted from without or within, but the corruption from without stems from society's incessant teachings to us of "our" vulgarity, violence, and sexually deviate behavior. The corruption from within stems from these teachings which have been taught to our ancestor's and it has been passed on through centuries, along with poverty, ignorance and inequality of this country.

This country's morality is the structure of its culture and its culture has been adopted and adapted by us; to our detriment. We must hate those catastrophic ideologies and until we hate them we will never defeat them. A single deed of oppression could be accredited to a mistaken belief of the time, but consistent series of oppressive, despotic acts, starting at a specific point and sought consistently through every administration throughout this country's history, this demonstrates an intentional plot to reduce and continue with the reduction of our mental and physical state. This relegates us to another form of slavery today.

Slavery far exceeds the definition most are familiar with. However, our perception of it has been distorted since the "emancipation of proclamation" was signed by Abraham Lincoln. There exists more to our "emancipation" than what many have been taught; it's not surprising. Lincoln didn't have an overwhelming compassion of the plight of African slaves. His decision was based on Politics. We need to be aware of these things, yet most historians fail to discuss it; the frequency at which the dominant class and those whom it serves, goes about bringing to fruition their ideas in policies.

Our "emancipation" was the collateral effect to the things going on at the time of this documents signing. Lincoln wrote a letter to Horace Geely stating, "My paramount object in this struggle (civil war) is to save the Union, and is not either to save or destroy slavery. If I could save the Union without freeing any slave, I would do it; and if I could save it by freeing all the slaves, I would do it; and if I could do it by freeing some and leaving others alone, I would also do that."

The North (Union) and South (Confederate) had different ideas with slavery being one. The North and South were collectively considered the Union, but the South wanted to secede from the Union and declare sovereignty over themselves, controlling their own profits from slavery and other endeavors. As from this letter Lincoln wrote in 1852, it demonstrates his indifference to our ancestors' ordeals during slavery. Historically, we have many speeches authored by Lincoln designed to portray him as a staunch advocate of the abolishment of slavery. The personal letter he wrote demonstrates his real attitude towards the African slaves. Lincoln was a politician and as such, he would have said what was necessary to be elected or stay in office, so if a virtue has to be created or compromised, it usually is done. He very well may have felt "bad" at slavery's cruelty, but not to the extent of abolishing it without his political agenda.

We may have benefitted from the "emancipation of proclamation" but it wasn't the deciding factor. Sadly, many of our clergy of today are just as willing to compromise as are politicians and this in turn further subjugates many of our people to more unconsciousness. They are prepared to compromise for popularity, monetary or political agendas. It seems that wealth and pleasure have numbed our minds and hearts to a point that God's priorities of social advancement and consciousness of Him and ourselves have become unwelcomed. We can survive foolishness, to a degree, even adamant fools, but we cannot survive betrayal from within; like an enemy at the gate like the Visigoths at the conquering of Rome in 410 A.D. An enemy is observed and shows open hostility, but a traitor slyly sabotages from within those gates.

I am strongly against religious leaders compromising their faith for a fear of public perception. This leaves communities spiritually and socially handicapped more so than they already are. The fact is that society at large is known for compromising, not just their religious or political figures. All of the leaders are susceptible to compromise and some make it a habit to do so. I can't begin to imagine the pressures they are constantly under and   I'm surely not automatically implying hypocrisy or unfaithfulness, but compromise is a subtle and potentially destructive trait.

One of the most extreme examples of compromise that I could think of is of Pontius Pilate acquiescing to the crowds' desire to execute Yeshua ("Jesus"), even though Pilate found no evidence of wrong doing. He even told the would-be Persecutors he had no fault in Him. (Matthew Chapter 27). Even after this declaration, the crowd persisted, "Let him be crucified." Pilate washed his hands and claimed that he was innocent of Christ's death, though he being the Roman Governor had sole authority over who was to live or die; Romans alone had the power to sanction a death sentence. He knew Christ did nothing worthy of death, but for the sake of his political career, he sentenced him to death. His principles and ethics were disregard for the sake of appeasing his crowds.

Religious leaders of today may not compromise to such a fatal degree, at least an obvious one, but their results can sometimes be just as catastrophic. Just because the affects maybe hidden a little better, this does not mean they are any less fatal. The man who refuses to compromise will have many enemies, but a clear conscience is his reward and a great ally, but sadly many don't seem to care for that. How can we professing men of faith be responsible to God, if we're irresponsible to our brothers? Are they not made in His image? We must strive to be true to God and ourselves because if we aren't true to one, how could we be really true to the other?

To become conscious is to realize that the spiritual is truly stronger than the physical and that it can decide the physical, if aptly applied. All that we do is still much less than that which remains to be done, but it must be done. What are we doing that will outlast our physical being? We can't allow for our eyes to believe everything that it visually sees, or our ears to believe everything it audibly hears. This causes so much to be believed, even in error. We must become conscious of our capacity for righteousness, not just for depravity. This society instills such negativity in us that we've allowed for its perpetuation subconsciously to guide us.

We must become aware of our responsibility to awaken our self beyond the initial emotion of feelings that accompany consciousness. We can use those emotions as a catalyst, whether it's of the constant injustices we see committed against our people or an encounter with knowledge revealing them. We must transition from ignorance to illumination. It would be irresponsible for me to not further expound on Lincoln's ideology toward African slaves.

Three years prior to Lincoln's presidency, he continued to express indifference towards our people. " I will say then that I am not, nor have I ever been, in favor of bringing about in anyway the social and political equality of the black races-that I am not, nor ever have I been, in favor of making voters or jurors of negroes, nor of qualifying them to hold office, nor to intermarry with white people…and in as much, they cannot so live, while they remain together, there must be a position superior and inferior and I as much as any other man am in favor of having the superior position assigned to the white race." These are not the words of a Negro "savior" as history would have us believe. In fact, it shows that he compromised what he believed by signing the "emancipation of proclamation."

He also stated "He always hated slavery as much as the abolitionist, but he never intended to do anything about it where it exists." It was so appropriately stated by Ed Burke that "the only thing needed for evil to triumph is for good men to do nothing." His goodness could be debated by his observations of such cruelty and his authority to intervene much sooner, not out of spite towards the Confederate Army, but a compassion for humanity that the African slaves have. But his entire presidential platform in 1860 was that he wouldn't interfere with slavery where it existed. Prior to his first term on December 20, 1860, South Carolina and several other Southern States seceded to form the Confederate States of America because they feared action was certain, and with it, the eradication of slavery.

Clearly, they had not paid attention to the constant attempt of Lincoln that he had no intention towards abolishing slavery. He tried to convince the Southern states that "the abolishing of slavery was wrong because the promulgation (a decree) of abolition doctrines tend to rather increase than to abate the evils of slavery." The Southern states disbelieved and chose to be the aggressors of the Civil War by firing the 1st shot at Fort Sumner on April 12, 1861; even after Lincoln (again) on March 4, 1861 said "I have no purpose, directly or indirectly, to interfere with the institution of slavery in the states where it exists." He even held up the "Fugitive Slave Act" providing that runaway slaves be returned to their "owners." So it stands to reason, the "emancipation" was signed out of spite by Lincoln.

All of the concessions offered to the South were at our expense. So, in July 1862, he laid plans to his cabinet for the purpose of retaliation against the South. It ("emancipation of proclamation") was finalized in January 1, 1863 freed slaves ONLY in the Southern areas where the confederacy was still in rebellion, not in the Southern areas where the Union army was occupied or loyal slave states. His Secretary of State, William H. Seward, called the "emancipation" document deplorable and was aghast at Lincoln's intent by stating, "We show our sympathy with slavery by emancipating them where we cannot reach them and holding them in bondage where we can set them free."

Yet, Lincoln made no mistake about what his intentions were, he stated "What I do about slavery and the colored race, I do because it helps save the Union." Historians portray Lincoln the "Great Emancipator," a moral and compassionate man of Africans, but the fact remains that he was an astute Politician. He may have felt "bad" about the plight of the slaves, but had it not been for the zealousness of the confederate Army, slavery still would have existed during his term as President. The fact that his political agenda superseded our well being; this is a common problem of today. Though we benefitted from it, it was not done for our benefit.

Lincoln's conclusion to the Civil War was just as hypocritical as his whole reason for our "emancipation." One of the last confederate General's (Lee) surrendered and Lincoln suggested that the south would be allowed to "slowly" be allowed to give up their slaves. Five years time was what they were given. This was only because the newly ratified 13th Amendment which abolished slavery was signed, but the Southern (Confederate states) would be given millions of dollars in government compensation for the release of their slaves. The argument could very well be made that Lincoln merely bought slaves himself. This act shows that Lincoln's concern was really about the union and the white men he felt were superior to African slaves.

The majority of these facts are absent from our children's history books and the sad reality is that when our children grow into adulthood, they are totally unconscious of the true characteristics of individuals who they have been taught to honor. If we are ignorant of our history, clearly our future cannot be expected to be one of consciousness if we don't seek it. So much of our history has been lost simply because we're not the author's of it in respects to the "History" taught in American schools. We have been systematically belittled with our roles in the global historical significance we possess.

Not many people are aware that at the time of World War II, there were at least 24,000 Native Africans in Germany. They had been there because Germany established colonies in Africa in the late 1800's in Togo, Cameroon, Namibia and Tanzania. Their genetic experiments began and most were on African prisoners. This left 60,000 dead. Following a 4 year revolt against the German colonization, Germany was stripped of its African colonies in 1918 after their defeat in World War I. As a spoil of war, France occupied Germany in Rhineland estate that has gone back and forth between the two for centuries.

France deployed their own colonized Africans as the occupying force and Germany soon voted for the Nazi party with a staggering 92% of the vote. This was because they perceived the Africans occupying their land as the final insult. Hundreds of African Rhineland-based soldiers intermarried with German women and raised their children as African Germans. Hitler wrote in his book "Mein Kampf" (My Battle), his plans for these "Rhineland bastards." Upon obtaining power, he made it his priority to deal with mixed-race children. In 1937, every identified mixed child in the Rhineland had been forcibly sterilized to prevent more "race pollution"; this was Hitler's belief.

They were given no anesthetic and only received a sterilization certificate, so long as they agreed to have no sexual relations with German women, according to Hans Hauck (African Holocaust survivor and sterilization survivor). Most African Germans had tried to escape Germany to France but were unable to because nations had prohibited Germans to enter, especially African Germans. Many did choose to stay in Germany, mistakenly placing their nationality as a primary. Some even foolishly fought with the Nazi's but this stemmed from an unconsciousness which is more pathetic than it is uncommon.

Many, many others were however, arrested and charged with treason and shipped to concentration camps. These trains were similarly packed like the slave ships which brought us to America. And just as the Trans Atlantic slave trade proved fatal, so did the four day journey for many of the German Africans." They were accompanied with African soldiers from the U.S. Army, and then starved while forced to work dangerous jobs, all of which violated the Geneva Convention. (Document signed by the main countries dictating the way war prisoners should be treated) Many of the "'German Africans" were forced to man the crematoriums, disposing of corpses and test subjects themselves. They were killed every ten months so they wouldn't be able to reveal Hitler's inner workings of his "Final Solution," which was the total eradication of the Jewish people.

There were Africans who resisted Hitler, such as Lari Gilges who founded Northwest Rann - an organization of entertainers who fought the Nazi's in his home town of Dussel Dorf and he was murdered in 1933, the same year Hitler took power of Germany, rather the year his power was solidified. According to Delroy Simms of Essex University, "Little information remains about the exact number of "African Germans" who had been held in the camps and killed, but some of Nazi sterilization survivor's are still alive and their story is told in "Black Survivor's of the Nazi Holocaust." They speak out for justice, not for history. Unlike the Jews in Israel and Germany, "African Americans" received no reparations of war because their citizenship was revoked by Hitler.

These instances of past and present scenarios demonstrate a clear, regardless of what country we're in, demonstration of our mistreatment. It's compounded by the fact that everyone wants for us to remain ignorant of these acts. It seems that the only justice that we can get is to raise the consciousness of our children in order for them to know what exactly, and how subtle our enemies are. To further add injury to insult, the surviving "African Germans" who did survive were wound up and tried as war criminals. Much of the complete picture of our history has been diluted to a point of disbelief to many Native Africans once they hear of it. Sadly, they've bought in to the mistaken belief that what the Caucasian teacher in school teaches them, it's to be believed unquestioned.

Many are unable to accept the fact that they've been taught erroneously and if we continue to use this ideology that we've been taught, we will NEVER come from underneath the unconsciousness which blankets our people. Then we automatically believe all others and distrust our own people, for no reason other than their heritage, we minimize any progress of our potential accomplishments it will be even more difficult, not to mention hindering us from finding the correct answers to problems which have been plaguing us for decades, even centuries.

Obviously, we must face obstacles before we could appreciate our victory, so when we need to overcame opposition, it will indicate our determination and perseverance, despite the conflict aimed at us. The more perplexing the problem, the more value the solution holds.

Unfortunately, our current way of existence seems to have fed us complacency, so devastating, that our condition worsens, despite the fact many believe it improves. The fact that we've adapted to the subconscious, unconsciousness threatens our future because of the "information" we've been given and hold on to while accepting that no conscious designs have been established in order for us to alter our current misery. One must ask, do we enjoy seeing ourselves like this? Or do we not care?

Everything that we do (collectively and individually) is a demonstration of our degree of consciousness or unconsciousness. What is the difference between anything from one person to the next? The main difference is their individual perception of the object. Take for example an individual who makes $20,000 a year and give him a check for that amount, he literally will feel as if he's won the lottery and hopefully, he'll be grateful for the gift. Now, take an individual who earns a million dollars a year and give the same $20,000 and he probably will feel insulted, maybe indignant, even if he does take the check. The $20,000 can buy the same thing for the one as it could for the other.

Yet, the standard of living will probably be different, so the individual who earns a million a year merely sees that money as a down payment on merely one luxury item, but the individual who earns only $20,000 can pay off bills and potentially get them self something nice. I'm sure he'll use it more efficiently than his counterpart. The point is that only their perception is different of the same exact thing - $20,000 dollars. We may all have varying opinions of $20,000, but we need to be on one accord regarding the necessity of our youth to be properly educated with a sense of consciousness of our heritage.

This will help our progression.

Yet, sadly many don't value our youth, this in turn continues to be noticeable to our youth, who often seek their value through drugs, sex, or a plethora of other destructive vices, which in turn further destroy our communities. We can't argue that we have not in turn allowed for genocide to run our streets.

Subconsciously Unconscious

CHAPTER 4
Teacher Teach Us

The mis-education our youth are subjected to goes beyond the school system in which we trust their learning to, but the mis-education we ourselves give them, or allow for them, to obtain from the streets, or entertainment industry, is just as detrimental as anything we allow for them to be taught in school. Mis-education suppresses logic given characteristics and if we aren't allowing ourselves to be productive for God and our communities; we'll inevitably be instruments for destruction for our communities. There is no room on the side lines when dealing with the well being of our youth. This battle in our communities forces all of us (it should) to be active in this fight because of all of the years of inactivity we've seen, we can see the results.

There exists misguided ones in our communities, rather in our heritage because they've left our communities LONG AGO. They have become indifferent to our Native African youth, choosing to belittle the reality of systematic racism, classism, and hypocrisy which have all had numerous negative effects on our people.

To those who deny their posterity, they don't deserve the posterity that God gave them. We may very well have to allow for them to stand as they choose; relegating them to opposition. I don't mean to imply we shouldn't diligently try to enlighten them, but we can't allow for their willful choice of unconsciousness to deter us from doing what we need to do, which is to unify ourselves.

We must never forget the reason for which we take up such a daunting task; it's necessary. This is to ensure that our youth will at least have a fighting chance. We've had many pioneers in the past fighting for our advancement, and though they utilized various methods, they sought a common goal: a fair treatment of Africans and their descendants. From Frederick Douglas and his attempt at abolishing slavery, Nat Turner and his attempt at freeing slaves, and Dr. Martin L. King and his attempt to bring to fruition the alleged "constitutional rights" we purported to possess.

The argument could be made that they each failed and accomplished, with respects to their endeavors, but it's beyond question that they tried with all of their heart to achieve it.

Because of their tenacity, we're able to stand on their shoulders because of the success that they did receive, but we seem content on not allowing for our children to be granted this same gift. It seems that we push them away from our past accomplishments, expect for them to succeed without our guidance, and then are shocked at the massive wrong choices that they make. Can we really be surprised at the fact that they gravitate towards negativity when we're non-responsive of their TRUE academic and historical needs? No one can accurately cite the exact number of gang members in this country, but not many (if any) would argue that Native Africans and Hispanics comprise of the majority. Our youth find it easy to identify with other, seemingly, abandoned youth. This compounded with poverty and frustration at the educational system for the constant barrage of half truths given to them. Our youth aren't as easily manipulated, so they act out in erroneous ways which only further perpetuates unconsciousness.

This has positive and negative results; the positive is that they aren't willing to be mislead, so they presume their teachers are less than truthful and they want to know the truth, but in their disbelief of their teacher's they relegate their parent's to the same "lying authority figure," simply because the parent's tend to mimic whatever the teacher says as valid. This is primarily because the parents themselves don't know any better. When our youth are allowed to possess idle minds, they become mentally weakened and susceptible to believe whatever the latest entertainer speaks. We have basically facilitated idleness in our youth, not to mention our adults as well. Not only have we facilitated it, but we've idolized negativity because it's such a common occurrence in our communities.

Some will never obtain any massive degree of empowerment because of the negatives images, which makes it easier for us to be mentally weakened. We must be adamant in our desire to change negative images into positive aspirations. We have nothing against us that is too strong that it can't be broken off if we are willing to fight for what we know is at risk; our youth. We must be careful not continue to allow for others to determine our destiny with hopes of their kindness of their beliefs. We can change much of our collective ideologies if we're willing to go to a place where we seek consciousness instead of comfort. This will have to be done in increments, but it HAS to be done.

Our current state needs a severe alteration and this will have to be sparked by our collective will for change. A will to do something isn't the same as a will to change mental states. The latter is more difficult. We cannot continue to allow for our emotional and psychological stability to be established by false western concepts because they propagate a defeatist mentality in us. So often we accept or reject a belief based on a ingrained presumption, due to what we have heard, been taught or assumed without any type of validation of the concept. The main predicament we find ourselves in is massive unconsciousness.

Why do so many people believe what they've gotten from the media or their teachings from school in this western society and ask so few questions and hold on to the information so enthusiastically? Many choose to allow for themselves to believe in things for convenience, maybe for traditional purposes without pondering what damage these beliefs may cause, to either their well being or their consciousness. Our conscious directed thought can yield positive results, if we deliberately aim our efforts at achieving them. We've been oppressed for so long by so many it (convenience or tradition) ought never dictate anything again.

There exists another practice, which so blatantly inviolate our youths worth that the failure of our people to recognize or speak out about it is shameful to all people in this country, not just Native Africans. We've all seen the misfortunate parents on the news agonizing over the disappearance of their child, as we should empathize with those parents over the loss of a child; we fail to ever question why we seldom see news coverage at the disappearance of Native African children. Some may question how I could make such a sad ordeal racial, but I don't make it racial, I simply expose the racist practices in the media.

In 2006 the F.B.I. reported that 33% of 700,000 children missing yearly were "African American." It reveals that more of our children missing more frequently than we may have known. How could we know when the media coverage is so inept, or at the least indifferent to their disappearance? I'm sure that many are familiar with the names Elizabeth Smart, Chandra Levy, Amber Hagerman and Jessica Lunsford, just to name a few. If they aren't familiar with then, I'm sure they could easily locate dozens of past newspaper articles on them. The national "Amber Alert' was named after Amber Hagerman. Jessica Lunsford's death increased the penalties for sex offenders in Florida, which soon found itself nationwide. In mid 2007, the magazine "News Week" included these cases in a story whose headlines spoke volumes: "Abductions that changed America." Out of the 8 cases profiled, each one abducted during a 33 year span was Caucasian.

The message was not as subtle as previously believed, and the message is the same as it's always been: our lives are of less value than Caucasians. In fact, the majority of the time the only time native African children receive coverage is when the parents are a suspect. A sad case is a single mother named Janet Harris from New Jersey, who in 2002 had been arrested for child endangerment and neglect because of her three year old son's right broken leg and despite a geneticist's professional opinion that her son Jyrene suffered from osteogenesis imperfecta - a serious genetic disorder meaning "imperfectly formed bones." His last break was the fourth in two years. She was in jail at the time of his kidnapping and stayed there two months after the medical report validated his injuries were not caused by his mother.

Janet Harris spent a total of six months in jail. His kidnapping occurred 13 days prior to Elizabeth Smart's, but nothing in the media would have indicated the disappearance of this three year old "African American" child. His abduction occurred like Elizabeth Smart's, abducted at home from his bed and only $1000 was raised by the Essex county prosecutor for Jyrene. Ms. Smart's parents were already on NBC and CNN pleading for the return of their child, rightfully so, plus over 200 volunteers searching high and low for Ms. Smart. A $10,000 reward had grown into a $250,000 reward and the Utah's West desert was covered with 55 A.T.V.'s looking for Ms. Smart.

Essence magazine found that there were more than 13,000 newspaper articles from 2002-2007 discussing Elizabeth Smart, and a mere 42 mentioning Jyrene, and only seven of those were complete stories. The main gist of those articles was that his mom was to blame for his disappearance, even though she was in jail at the time of his abduction. To further insult the situation, the F.B.I. still viewed her suspiciously after her release from jail, so they gave her a lie detector test. It's hard to imagine the pain of having a child kidnapped, then to be accused of having it done from jail, this has the potential to make even the most stable minded person have a mental breakdown; this just is one more example of the value attributed to our lives.

There were no billboards for Jyrene, no donations or media coverage to solicit donations to help increase the chance of his recovery, no search parties - just a tortured mother and a biased police investigation focusing on her prematurely, which undoubtedly allowed for the real assailant to go undetected. According to Donald Hampton, a executive director of Washington D.C. based National Black Police Association, "Black life doesn't appear to have the same value that white life has." This sentiment has reigned for 100's of years in this country, not to mention other countries. There's a real disparity in the treatment of missing "African Americans" than that of Caucasians. Alonzo Wash spoke it so correctly when he stated, "The darker you are, the poorer you are, the less likely you are to get media attention." (Alonzo Wash, Community Activist)

As painful as these demonstrations are, the blatant nature of these incidents still have people unconscious as the devalued status of our children is propagated. They've received so many messages invalidating their worth, on so many different levels, that it seems irreversible. It's tragic, deplorable, and even heart wrenching to know that if any of our children turn up missing they have only a 10-15% chance of the media giving them any substantive coverage at all, while their Caucasian counterparts receive the remainder of the coverage. These types of ordeals we have been forced to deal with are only a fraction of the problems we must overcome.

Our unconsciousness and unwillingness to address these situations need to be changed, I don't mean to sound cynical, but we've had too many instances where our worth has been minimized for us to not consider it as anything other than what it is; deliberate.

We can't keep complacent in ignorance, because that will not aid us in altering what needs to be altered; not only the effects this has on our communities, but the causes as well. It can't be argued that our lack of conscious is a main cause of our current state. Without an opportunity, our abilities will be wasted. And without abilities, our opportunities will arise in vain. Obviously, if we aren't prepared to take the sole responsibility of our consciousness, despite its common lacking, we will continue to be subconsciously oppressed, mostly by our own doing.

We can be sure that any introduction to new ideas will meet with resistance and opposition from those who benefit from our being in this current dismal state, but opposition from those who should be glad to see their heritage raise itself up from the tumultuous state should be nonexistent and anyone who goes into this half heartedly will be just as much of a distraction as opposition. These half hearted individuals have that attitude due to a fear of the daunting scale of problems which they (we) face, a subconscious belief that it will fail. Some men lack faith in anything until it's been proven to wok. Throughout history man has always opposed roads where the possibility of difficulty will be great, but we are much better off attempting feats of excellence for our people, than to wallow in the sub-humane present day reality we face.

Simply because other heritages believe that they are superior than ours doesn't make it true, just like the fact that we've been taught lies through the years does not make them true either simply because we believe them. Virtually every other heritage feels that their heritage is superior to Africans, and though we may never answer this question out loud, is this why we feel as if we're less than everyone else? Many may disagree with that, but our levels of genocide, and atrocity committed by us on us, clearly this states differently.   By our present way of life, what we're saying is that we've adopted and accepted from the past experiences, the false and constantly perpetuated false information regarding us.

We also state that we have no desire to change. We must get to the mental position of destroying the past which is affecting our present. Our future will be comprised of what we have confidence in- there's no difference between things except our perception of its value. (This is a world based on external focus). Everything that we do in this life is a reflection of the level of consciousness that we possess and the value that we place in ourselves. We must take the knowledge that already exists and convert it into consciousness. Sadly, the first reaction to truth when it's not what we expected or desire is to deny it.

We're in denial about this revelation that almost everything they've taught us in school is wrong, or at the least half of the story. If we continue trying to make things work with the information that we've received from school, the results we desire will never materialize. Despite all the confusion and failure in our lives, we don't attempt to do anything differently today than from yesterday: this could be labeled insanity. We have the power to complete our thoughts by combining them with other thoughts, creating an idea, which can potentially create beneficial results. What we create from within will always be mirrored without. In other words, what we focus on will be our objective.

Many of us have heard that there are three types of people in the world: those who make things happen, those who watch things happen, and those who wonder what happened. We must be the former because we can't sit and watch and hope things will get better and we definitely can't sit and wonder what has happened, all the while ignoring the further descent we've fell into. If no one else is, we are responsible for the change which we so desperately need in our communities. We must not doubt our success just because of how daunting the tasks seems. Doubt precipitates chaos, which stifles potential advancement of any cause. It prevents from solving problems. It makes it virtually impossible to change conditions and with a doubtful attitude, we're unable to successfully dictate the future generations of our youth.

The hazard with doubt is that it causes for you to doubt and go against God's will. This rejects who you (we) truly are. And in rejecting our self, how can we really have confidence in the righteous endeavors we seek? We can never believe that we must settle for things the way that they currently are, nor must we think that even if we are successful at elevating our self higher, we must just stay at that position. We must never seek to be content with progress; we must always be in a state of progression. Yet, the information that we learn is VITAL to our consciousness.

The brain is made to respond to the printed word on a much deeper level than it is wired to respond to an audible one. There is no substitute for reading, but what you read dictates your thoughts. The expansion of one's vocabulary leads to a greater range of words one is able to command, and this is going to determine what we can achieve. The words we use will shape our thoughts just like the words we read (or listen to) will. Anytime something is made in a certain way and for a certain purpose, yet it acts against its nature, it hastens its demise. This is EXACTLY what is happening with the "African Americans" today.

Words express our thoughts, so we must develop an ability to express ourselves properly in order to help us obtain what it is that we all should want for our future generations: consciousness. Not to fail to mention the fairness which will increase once we're all on one accord, in respects to what it is we crave for our children. We must realize that the desire to change isn't the same as the will to change, but we must also know that the belief in some things doesn't necessarily make that belief true. As a result, our lives are dominated by our behavior. The lack of self consciousness is due to an under-developed will, which is the reason so many of us know to do better, but are unwilling to.

Our failure to act on that knowledge prevents us from obtaining wisdom. Wisdom is basically knowledge converted into actions, as opposed to just knowing bits of information. It's long overdue for us to stop accepting false teachings that this society perpetuates to any unconscious enough to believe it. Sadly, it's primarily our people who have been deceived; rather we suffer the most detriment from this deception. The future generations of our children are dependant mostly on the education they receive in this country's public schools, but as history demonstrates that factual accounts aren't all that is needed.

If our children continually see negative depictions of themselves in the media, or given only a portion of the contributions we've made globally, they will continue to behave as if they can't contribute anything, with the exception of sports and entertainment. We will not see them progress in a substantial manner. Before any structure takes form, a foundation must be set, and it must be set well enough to sustain the structure, otherwise the same thing will happen to our youths if the foundation isn't well prepared; it will collapse at the weight of the structure (idea). We have to realize that as long as we allow unconsciousness to be the normal behavior, this will continue to diminish the potential our youth.

This fails to mention their competence, their performance and their all around self-esteem. This will cause further negative ideas to spark from them about themselves. Society already depicts them as not being as qualified as others. We must be mindful to instill in them their potential for excellence, and let them know that a failure doesn't make them a failure. "To err is human." We must teach them that perseverance has many lessons, so they can't be inclined to give up at the sign of difficulties which will lie ahead. It has never been a shock that we (Native Africans) have to work twice as hard just to get to the same position that others are starting from. For some odd reason, many people (Caucasians and "African Americans" believe that prejudices and racism has all but disappeared.

This truthful, albeit racist comment from former Georgia school superintendent Gustuvas R. Glenn stated "The colored man will only be a danger to us when we leave him to be educated by outside philanthropist-you need not be afraid of the Negro boy. It will take him a thousand years to get where your boy is." His statement simply means that anyone (philanthropist) teaching in contradiction to the western society's ideals, that is the only thing to threaten the current positions of Caucasians. He knew that we (Native Africans) will only be at our best when we're taught differently than we presently are. I don't agree that it will take 1000 years, but I do believe, no, I know, it will take a re-education of our people.

I don't imply that Caucasian children aren't also suffering from the inept schooling of this country, but it's indisputable that we are suffering far worse than others. They have no need to worry about us competing with them, not as long as we demonstrate belligerence on such a massive scale. It's self-evident by the constant showing that our lives are de-valued; from the way we treat each other, to the way others treat us- not to fail to mention the way society treats us in general. And the complacency of our plight is troubling. The ways in which we demonstrate our unconsciousness is vast, but no one is so conscious that he can't be taught something else. Lies have many entrances, but no exits; only truth will release us.

With all of the beliefs that I write in regards to our children needing to be taught by us, this doesn't absolve them from the responsibility of their choices. Yet, it's difficult to make wise choices when you've only been taught how to make bad ones. It's our duty to awaken our youth, not to mention ourselves, to our capabilities and stop expecting for anyone else to. We've become our own worst enemy, but we should be and can be our greatest ally.

A lack of economic dependence isn't the only reason were in this position; in fact our unconsciousness can very well be the cause of our poverty stricken communities. We just don't wish to strive to grab a hold of the things that everybody wants for their youth: a better life.

A constant stream of unreliable leader's, negative inferiority complexes propagated by this western society and a lack of consciousness ravage our people. Why would we expect proper teaching from those who benefit off our ignorance? When we learn to really love ourselves, then we'll be willing to teach ourselves. To some, this may be only words, but to those who care about our future-this is LIFE AND DEATH. When "in the course of human events, it becomes necessary for one people to dissolve the political bands which have connected them with another, to assume among the powers of earth the separate and equal station to which the laws of nature of God entitles them, a decent respect to the opinions of mankind requires they should declare the causes which impel them to separation." Declaration of Independence.

This is no less true for "African Americans" than it was for the country's slave owning "founding fathers." Our separation from this country isn't a new concept, many fail to realize that the very government virtually practices separation with the laws which they implement, or at the least the treatment they allow to be used against us. If we have an entire country to virtually fight off, then it makes no sense for us to continue to fight each other in the process.

The 19th century author and historian, Lydia Child recognized a truth so poignant, that despite its age, it still rings true; "Slaves have stabbed themselves for freedom-jumped into the ocean for freedom-fought like wild tigers for freedom! But they have been hung, burned, and shot and their tyrants have been their historians." (1843) With that being recognized of our heritage, how many of us are even willing to sacrifice merely a few luxuries? We mustn't forget that this is for a goal too important to disregard-our children. Liberty won't come until we're unified, and we won't become unified until we develop consciousness of the systematic divisions set against us.

The governmental structure of today is content with the poor being driven into further poverty, while the rich increase in wealth. Sadly, we've become accustomed at being poor and ignorant, which is a main cause of our divisive nature. The times call for us to be as blatant in our assessments of our condition and as uncompromising as God while He deals with sin. We must stop accepting different versions of freedom; one people believe that they have the right to pursue life, liberty, and the pursuit of happiness and to work enjoying the fruits of their labor, while another group believes they have the right to enjoy the fruits of THOSE people's labor and to do with those people as they wish.

They have contrived a false notion of "freedom," because in actuality it's oppression. And they will continue to succeed as long as we're divided. The need for self help is the root of true growth for our people; it demonstrates determination, which is what we need in order to counter the attacks which are constantly sat against us. Help from outside of our community (heritage) usually is insufficient, or misguided, but self determination of a unified people has the creativity to orchestrate change. How can we think that we individually can enjoy equality and freedom unless we all do?

This country will never be a free one until its inhabitants that are poor are able to enjoy the same liberties that the rich people enjoy. "If a free society refuses to assist those unable to help themselves, we cannot expect to do so for the wealthy when they need it." (John F. Kennedy) Inequality has the tendency to enrich our upper class, dehumanize our middle class and further impoverish our lower class. "There are at least two things we have a right to...death or liberty." (Harriet Tubman). I can only see liberty by our being unified; this will encourage and strengthen us.

Unification will cause for us to attempt things beneficial to our people's plight, regardless to who approves or disapproves of it. We must be willing to educate ourselves, because in this effort at consciousness, we'll be better situated to raise the conscious of our youth. Our communities have the potential to soar, like an airplane, but even in the event of the "pilot's" death, a "co-pilot" should be ready to take the proverbial wheel of leading in our communities. If we're going to be totally honest, for every person who rose up speaking against the harsh treatment of "African Americans," the majority were met with either a political or actual assassination. I know that I am not the only one tired of seeing our people on their backs, talking about how tragic it is that we are in the current position, yet not doing anything to change it.

Our actions have consequences, just as any inaction on our part will continue to current cycles we're seeing played out in our communities. It isn't our wealth which determines our liberty or existence, but our existence is determined by our being conscious of everything that we have to face as a people. "The descendants of enslaved African's have an entirely different experience than those of different races in America." (Dorothy Tillman). Consciousness will spark a desire for true liberty. It's sad that we are holding our own communities "hostages" by our current behaviors; it's not like we don't have enough external forces oppressing us already.

America is notorious for "eating their young" people, yet so many of our people seemed surprised by these facts. According to the Sentencing Project 2009 (Ashley Nellis and Ryan King) "African Americans" comprise of 49.3% of inmates serving life without Parole, yet Caucasians merely 33.4%. How can we comprise of only 12% of the National percentage, while possessing nearly half of the people serving life sentences? This is just another subtle example of our value to this American society; sadly it also reflects an unwillingness of our people to pay attention to our treatment.

This reality seems to confront our people in ways that they don't want to be confronted. If we don't all become ready to deal with our situation as a people in this country, the situation will continue to deal with us as it has been-catastrophically. It is human nature to desire prosperity, and this is not to be criticized, but honored. However, we tend to invest in visible successes, not in the invisible (rather future returned) wealth, such as the raising of our youth's consciousness. We tend to equate success with cars, jewelry and material acquisitions, but not in our youth.

This country is established by the blood of our ancestor's, so freedom ought to be our most prized possession; sadly it's not. It seems to be the most elusive. Slavery of our ancestry needs to be constantly inside of the consciousness, of not only our youth, but of our adults as well. It's not needed to be remembered for us to obtain empathy but for us to always remember what this country did to subjugate us in the past, and what it's trying to do to keep us in another form of slavery; unconsciousness. That end result causes for a multitude of other problems to plague our communities.

In 2006 President George Bush Jr. extended the "African Americans" right to vote for a few more decades. The 1965 Voting Rights Act was signed by President Lyndon B. Johnson giving us the right to vote. It was not designed to give us the rights indefinitely. It has been extended under Reagan and Bush. The point worth mentioning is that we continually are at their mercy in respects to our voting rights. Caucasians don't have to get their rights to vote extended, women don't have to get their right to vote extended, even legal immigrants don't have to get their right to vote extended, but "African Americans" do. Sometimes the most blatant statement is made in silence.

We have been here since approximately 1555 and yet our right to vote is under the discretion of the presidents. How is it most of our "African American" politicians seem content to not attempt to argue this injustice? We're collectively guilty of being "lulled" to a false comfort zone, which even the realization isn't hidden that we aren't doing too well in this country and this has been the case for centuries. America isn't totally to blame because she is what she has always been, with respects to "African Americans" on her soil.

We've not settled for a whole piece of the proverbial pie, but merely a piece of a piece of the pie, but this, in essence, is nothing. Most of us exist, either intellectually, physically, or morally, inside of a restrained sphere of our full potential. We use only a small amount of our possible consciousness; maybe we fear that once we become conscious, we'll really have to look at how we're devalued by this society, which in turn causes us to devalue ourselves.

I wonder would it take for the next time the extension of our voting rights are brought before a future president for his denial of them to manifest an awakening of our people. Maybe that act would reveal just how urgent a position that we're in; though I can't believe that the urgency of our situation isn't already shown.

Most don't understand the struggles that their facing have been orchestrated LONG before their birth. W.E.B. Dubois stated a crucial point when he said, "The cost of liberty is less than the cost of repression." Our freedom will only go as far as our consciousness takes us, and, by the looks of things presently, we can't get too far being, as a whole, unconscious. We need to adhere to three tactics: First, we are to desire consciousness of ourselves because no outside entity will attempt to raise our consciousness, so that is our responsibility. Secondly, we are to teach our youth, because if left to the current educational schooling, we'll continue to see the inferiority complexes that we've been seeing. Lastly, we must implement these difficult, but mandatory concepts. Obviously friction will surface.

I know that everyone isn't able to home school their children, but if we can teach them how to learn, we have the potential to alter the current situation our people are in. Anytime you fight the status quo, it will be confrontational. You've read some of the statistics, anytime we've gotten to a point that our status quo looks as it does now, we cannot afford to concern ourselves with who may or may not like our ideas of raising our consciousness.

Subconsciously Unconscious

CHAPTER 5
The Divided Conquerors

There is an ideology, so eerie that it defies logic as to how it seemingly has been followed to a degree of efficiency all to a detriment of Native Africans. Some choose to disbelieve the existence of Willie Lynch letters which is clearly an indication of a willful unconsciousness. These are not coincidences; these are his words and our plight is playing out exactly how he envisioned. These are his words uncensored and unaltered. Many are unfamiliar with the fact that Willie Lynch was a British slave owner whose name gave birth to the term lynch; everyone is familiar with that word's meaning. He advocated that all slave owners should use the tactics he implemented on his slaves and in 1712 in Virginia he was invited to a colony to teach them how to put them into practice. Here are his words:

"Gentlemen, I greet you here on the bank of the James River in the year of our Lord one thousand seven hundred and twelve. First I shall thank you, the gentlemen of the colony of Virginia for bringing me here. I am here to help you solve some of your problems with slaves. Your invitation reached me on my modest plantation in the West Indies where I have experimented with some of the newest and still oldest methods for control of slaves. Ancient Rome would envy us if my program is implemented. As our boat sailed south on the James River, named for our illustrious King, whose version of the Bible we cherish, I saw enough to know that your problem is not unique. While Rome used cords of wood as crosses for standing human bodies along its highways in great numbers, you are using the tree and the rope on occasion.

I caught a whiff of a dead slave hanging from a tree a couple miles back. You are not only losing valuable stock by hanging, you are having uprisings, slaves running away, your crops are sometimes left hanging in the field too long for maximum profit, you suffer occasional fires, your animals are killed, gentlemen you know what your problems are; I am here to introduce you to a method of solving them. I do not need to elaborate. I am not here to enumerate your problems. In my bag here, I have a fool proof method of controlling black slaves. I guarantee every one of you that if installed correctly, it would control the slaves for at least 300 years. My method is simple and members of your family and any overseer can use it. (We are approaching the 300th year in less than 2 years and still visual effects of his plan are demonstrated)

I have outlined a number of differences among the slaves; and I take these differences and make them bigger. I use fear, distrust and envy for control purposes. These methods have worked on my modest plantation in the West Indies and they will work throughout the South. Take this simple list of differences, think about them. On top of my list is "Age," but it is there only because it begins with "A." The second is "Color" or

"Shade," there is intelligence, size, sex, size of plantation, status of plantation, and attitude of owner, whether the slave lives in the valley, on a hill, east, west north or south, have a fine hair or course hair, or is tall or short.

Now that you have a list of differences, I shall give you an outline of action, but before I do that, I shall assure you that distrust is stronger than trust and envy is stronger than adulation, respect and admiration. (Author's interjection: These trivial differences are still prevalent in our psyche's, but with one newer addition; wealth. That very well maybe the most destructive difference we now have to deal with.)

"The Black slave, after receiving this indoctrination, shall carry on and will become self refueling and self generating for 100s of years, maybe thousands. Don't forget that you must pitch the old black vs. the young black and the young black male against the old black male. You must also use the dark skin slave vs. the light skin slave and the light skin slave against the dark skin slave. You must also have your white servants and overseers distrust all blacks, but it is necessary that your slaves trust and depend on us. They must love, respect and trust only us.

Gentlemen, these kits are keys to control, use them, have your wives and children use them, never miss an opportunity. My plan is guaranteed and the good thing about this plan is that if used intensely for one year, the slaves themselves will remain perpetually distrustful. Thank you, gentlemen." These ideals are tame in comparison to his writings "Let's make a slave" as recorded: "Let's make a slave. What do we need? First of all we need a nigger man, a pregnant nigger woman and her baby boy. Second, we will use the same basic principle that we use in breaking a horse combined with some more sustaining factors.

We reduce them from their natural state in nature; whereas nature provided them with their natural capacity to take care of their needs and the needs of their offspring, we break that natural string of independence from them and thereby create a dependency state so that we may be able to get from then useful production for our business and pleasure.

Cardinal principles for making a Negro for fear that our future generations may not understand the principles of breaking BOTH horses and men, we lay down the art. For, if we are to sustain our basic economy, we must break both of the beasts together; the nigger and the horse. We understand that short range Planning in economics result in periodic economic chaos, so that, to avoid turmoil in the economy, it requires us to have breadth and depth in long range, comprehensive economic planning:

1) BOTH MUST BE BROKEN and tied together for orderly production.

2) BOTH horse and niggers are no good to the economy in the wild or natural state.

3) For orderly futures, special and particular attention must be paid to the female and the youngest offspring.

4) BOTH must be cross bred to produce a variety and division of labor.

5) BOTH must be taught to respond to a peculiar new language.

6) Psychological and Physical instruction of containment must be created for both.

We hold the above six cardinals as truths to be self evident based upon the following discourses concerning the economics of the breaking and tying the horse and nigger together...all inclusive of the six principles laid down above.

NOTE: Neither principle alone will suffice for good economics. Accordingly, both a wild horse and a wild or natural nigger is dangerous even if captured, for they will have the tendency to seek their customary freedom, and in doing so, might kill you in your sleep.

You cannot rest. They sleep while you are awake, are awake while you are asleep.

They are dangerous near the family house and it requires too much labor to watch them away from the house. Above all, you cannot get them to work in this natural state. Hence, both the horse and nigger must be broken, that is breaking them from one form of mental life to another. Keep the body and take the mind. In other words, break the will to resist."

As diabolical as Willie Lynch's concepts for "breaking" the African seems, his ideals for our women are more sinister. "Therefore, if you break the female, she will break the offspring in its early years of development and when the offspring is old enough to work, she will deliver it up to you. For her normal female, protective tendencies have been lost in the original breaking process. Take the female and run a series of tests on her to see if she will submit to your desires willingly. Test her in every way, because she is the most important factor for good economics. If she shows any signs of resistance in submitting completely to your will, do not hesitate to use the bull whip on her to extract that last bit of bitch out of her.

Take care not to kill her, for in so doing, you spoil good economics. When in complete submission, she will train her offspring in the early years to submit to labor when they become of age. Therefore, we shall go deeper into this area of the subject matter concerning what we have produced here in this breaking of the female nigger. We have reversed the relationships. In her natural uncivilized state she would have a strong dependency on the uncivilized nigger male, she would have a limited protective dependency toward her male offspring and would raise female offspring to be dependant like her...with the male image destroyed the ordeal caused her to move from her psychological dependant state to a frozen independent state."

Willie Lynch further surmises, "Unless a phenomenon occurs and re-shifts the positions of the male and female savages, we will have an orbiting cycle that turns on its own axis forever." It is unquestionable that the 21st century plight of Native Africans demonstrates the subconscious effects in our mentality, which are largely due to the 19th century concoctions. Many of our people are unaware that learning from our past persecutions has the potential to aid us make better choices, utilizing the increased number of opportunities for our future generations, provided we're willing to awaken ourselves.

It is uncanny how such accuracies have played themselves out in our communities, not to mention eerie, yet the root cause can be the deception and the efficiency in which it has been propagated on our and by our ancestor's. An ignorance (unconsciousness) due to generations of mis-education, which has been hidden so well by the perpetrator's of the very lies which have yielded negative results, even hundreds of years later. This country's historical foundation has been rooted on the premise of subjugating and exploiting all non European (Caucasian) peoples , but it ESPECIALLY has been extremely successful at diminishing the consciousness of its African descendant's. The most shameful of that is that we have helped in perpetuating the division, jealousy and all out ignorance that has been grafted into us.

It could very well be said that when we give more concern to how we live, from an economical standpoint, than to our consciousness, we've forfeited the right to our very lives and their purposes. Some animals are instinctive by nature, with no concept of conscious or morality, but we often at times demonstrate more animalistic behavior when we disregard consciousness of God and self, not to fail to mention each other. This reduction of life causes for our lives as a whole, to be further diminished. Our situation will grow to a position of being no longer manageable or curable. How foolish are we to allow ourselves to be convinced that other groups of people know what needs to be done for us, or that they will do it.

A sad reality is that many of us fail to see that the solution to our community's afflictions lies in our very communities; such a lack of mental capacities on our part to accept truths that conflict with a current position of thought has the potentiality to devastate, either our minds or our position. Beliefs must change as our knowledge is increased. We must unlearn the errors in the concepts that we've been taught before we learn the truthful ones.

We should not allow a fear of offense or uncomfortability to believe new information and accept it after we've evaluated it to be true.

There are more important things in life instead of living solely to be in so called "comfort zones" because these very "comfort zones" have ravaged our psyches, which have ravaged our communities due to our failure to seek development of consciousness. It's well past a point of our needing to stop allowing for present circumstances (whether in poverty or financially wealthy) to determine our potential conditions on a conscious level. It is well worth reiterating that when we don't live seeking consciousness, but merely wealth than we don't deserve the wealth we may get if it's sought in a sacrifice of our future generations expense.

It is commonly considered divisive or "racist" whenever an "African American" speaks or attempts at challenging current conditions, by raising the conscious levels of his people. If we don't allow ourselves to unify on the basis of what we are, we will continually decline as a people. The reason our decline has been so prevalent is because throughout "American history," we've been taught subconsciously how to hate and devalue our own heritage. We won't be able to respect and love ourselves if our ancestry is hated and disrespected by our future generations. They feel as they do primarily because they've been taught that we've made no significant accomplishments prior to our "voyage" to the U.S.A. centuries ago.

One of the biggest shams is the so called "Black History Month," which only a few decades ago was merely "Black History Week." This deals primarily with the accomplishments of our people on this continent, and only for a mere 28 days. (Is it coincidence that it is in the shortest month of the year?) It rarely mentions the accomplishments of our people prior to our being kidnapped and sold to this country centuries ago. Without our pre-America experiences shown and taught to our children, they will continue to believe the media and error filled history taught to them. I truly believe that our judgment cannot be better than the information which we receive, so if we constantly see, and are constantly taught lies, we'll continue to see the results which we're seeing: unconsciousness.

These tactics seem almost invisible to a large portion of, of not only our children, but our adults as well. It's deplorable that in this "Age Of Information," we still find that many people aren't seeking, let alone concerned, with real African history.

If we fail to realize that our sub-conscious mind will react instinctively to what has been programmed into it-real or imagined - we will continue to see and behave as we do on the massive scale of unconsciousness, with massive scales of belligerence. The images of our self are based on this country's constant diet of negative and false information, so with this we continue to believe lies told to us about us. An unconscious mind cannot easily differentiate between the reality or false views of society.

We are primarily responsible for the proper educating of not only our future generations, but this must start with ourselves. It's indisputable that as more decades and centuries pass, the more valid the information is taken to be. Our contributions to humanity as a whole, is now not able to be completely disregarded by the prejudices of certain "scholars" ' "historians" who prior to the mid 1980's, attributed virtually everything worthwhile to Caucasian discovery or invention. It is unfathomable to believe that we'll advance as we need to in the future if we're unfamiliar with our past. Our present state clearly shows that we have serious flaws to rectify before we can TRULY advance socially.

"When you deal with the past, you're dealing with history; you're now dealing with actually, the origin of a thing. When you know the origin, you know the cause and if you don't know the cause, you don't know the reason" (Malcolm X). With our collective acceptance of failure to understand and discover our history and the contributions we made to it, we'll never excel in the future beyond what we're seeing. We must believe that the pursuit of consciousness is worth the effort and Pain needed to obtain it. We must re-discover who we are and what we are, if we don't, we run the risk of "psychological extinction" by our inaction. "Psychological extinction" simply means that we could become so callous about ourselves and the plight of our ancestors that we see only the now and some economic advancement made by a select few.

A few economic advancements will not eradicate the battle which has been taken place for centuries in the U.S. and most other countries across the globe. I speak plainly because it is much easier to be hated for who I am, than to be loved for someone who I am not.

Nothing can be done to alter the way we may be viewed by some, but we CAN alter the way we view ourselves. Our opinion of us is the most important opinion of us. I don't wish for people to think that I'm a separatist, but I simply expose that it exists, and not in so many subtle forms, but blatant ones as well. The sooner that people realize this, the sooner they can adapt and overcome its affects. Closure of one's eyes will not make the problem disappear, only a temporary blindness to it. But, even with closed eyes, the problem which was before them is still present. I refuse to accept the way things are in most of our communities as acceptable, so I strive for what I believe it could be: unified.

To have enough people who claim that they're "knowledged," but knowledge that isn't shared, doesn't do the unconscious ones any good. It's not what the society we live in tells us to do, but what our heritage, compassion and humanity tells us we ought to do.

This is the only way to at least guarantee that we'll have a chance at elevating socially, consciously, economically and globally. The liberty and justice that we've been lead to believe that we possess is, at best, a condensed version, or at worst, a false ruse told to us by this society's orchestrator's (politicians, teacher's etc). Liberty can't be preserved where people fail to recognize that it's missing. The conscious have the desire to know and seek truth, and they also desire to raise the consciousness of others.

The consequences are urgent and lasting, so to continue to be a willing participant in unconsciousness is beyond understanding. If we truly desire to be free from the chaos in our communities and if we truly desire to obtain the rights and liberty we've fought and died for, we must persevere to not forfeit the equality our enslaved ancestor's fought and died for. We must renew our vows to each other and stop allowing complacency to corrupt our consciousness. How could one expect to reap the benefits of consciousness if one isn't willing to fight for it? We have been operating without a true foundation based solely on false concepts and mistaken suppositions.

When I visualize of what we could become as a people, I see us raising ourselves up, but when we stay individually and collectively divided, we will continue to be defeated. A unified people are a powerful people to reckon with, yet we're often untrustworthy of each other that it contaminates any chances of us unifying for the collective advancement of our people. There exists many perils besides unconsciousness, but this has proven to be the most detrimental to our people than possibly any other mentality-even racism.

We must repay our ancestors, not to mention attempt to make it better for future generations. We must at least fight for the rights that they sacrificed themselves for; we can't expect for them (our posterity), to be a free people while they are an ignorant people. Instead of complaining about the way things are, we must resolve to change them. The unconsciousness isn't easily defeated, but the more difficult the battle, the more appreciated the victory. Many are under the mistaken assumption that they need to be motivated before they have to act, but once they act, it will surely spark the motivation which is needed. But let's be honest, how can anyone see the current state of "African Americans" today and not have a desire to alter their current position?

We should have a quest for consciousness and fairness which will empower us; this has been sought by our ancestors since our removal from Africa centuries ago. We must be treated fairly, benefitting from the liberty we as American born citizens possess. Or in the alternative, we must be willing to sacrifice whatever it is that's needed in order for it to be brought into fruition. Sadly, some of our people equate economic advancements as an indication of equality-it isn't. There ought not to be any emotion so strongly in our hearts than a desire for consciousness, which will spark a desire for true liberty.

We won't obtain true liberty until we unite on a scale so massive, that it cannot be ignored. God grants liberty, and those who love it must be willing to guard and defend it-to the death if need be. We can't obtain liberty in our communities until we unite. Liberty and unity are virtually inseparable.

CONCLUSION

I'm aware that there exist no simple solutions to the complex and deeply rooted problems, along with the society's deeply entrenched prejudices, which have proven so catastrophic to our people. I'm aware that no one book, not even a dozen, will automatically offset the century's long propaganda that we've been taught. The incessant struggles we see our people going through has created a defeatist attitude in our psyche's, causing us to believe that since the task is daunting, we don't even have to try and correct them. Too often we allow for the stigma that others place on us to be received as truth.

How come we've failed to realize that whoever controls our thoughts controls us? It's apparent that our consciousness isn't on anyone's agenda, so we may as well make it our priority. It is absolutely necessary that anything done for us will have to be done by us. It's sad to report that many of our people feel that we should amalgamate our culture and heritage to that of this Caucasian based society. The late Harold Washington stated so eloquently that "just because I love black people doesn't mean I hate everybody else." Surely we can seek for our children to be educated of their posterity without excluding the accomplishments of others.

If we continue breeding our children ignorant of our history, how could we expect for their future to be anything other than what we've been seeing? Have you ever noticed that trees without roots will soon die; so will a people without roots (cultural history) will too die; not all death is physical. I must reiterate why I consider us Native Africans, as opposed to "African Americans." I view us in terms of our ancestry, not our geography. Our lineage originated within the lands of Africa, so I feel more of a connection to that than to this American country. I don't critique my brothers and sisters for being proud of their American nationality, nor am I myself in opposition to mines, but my love for my forefathers supersedes my birthplace.

This is rather easy when you have a country, from its inception, which has done everything in its power to devalue my ancestor's. This has been done on a constant basis, with such efficiency that it still resonates within our communities hundreds of years later. If we're unwilling to alter some of our current concepts and beliefs, we'll never be able to alter our present day reality, as a side effect we'll never be able to rise above the misery we as "African Americans" have become accustomed to. We must believe that this is a vital undertaking, with that knowledge we must act in the same manner. We are defined by what we leave for them, God willing, we are desirous to leave it better than what we've witnessed.

The obstacles we must overcome are worth the reward we'll be able to leave our children. Humanity in general will benefit if we persevere and attempt to raise the consciousness of our children. But we must persist in the plans because without persistence, we invite failure. We owe this to them, we must be diligent in paying that debt. If we desire to truly educate our youth, it's obvious that we must inspire them. Ambition is not only a desire; it's a determination to achieve what you desire to come to pass. Sadly, many lack such a will and desire to become conscious and won't put forth the effort that it takes to accomplish such a mind state.

"When I discover who I am, then I'll be free" said the author Ralph Ellison, yet how many of our people feel that their freedom rests on their consciousness of themselves? Why do we insist on building our foundations on unstable ideals? Without us understanding our roles as Native African people, we'll never realize just how damaging that is to our youth. It could be argued that our allowance of a culture of inferiority has devastated us. Culture is merely a set of learned behaviors and ideals that we acquire as members of a certain country (or group), and this shows clearly that we pay attention to what has been taught to us. We all can probably agree that which we've been taught has been detrimental to our people.

The strength of any nation depends on solid familial bonds. Sadly, life and this book demonstrate just how weak the familial bonds are in this country, not just with our people, but with virtually every other people in this country. How can almost every other conquered society recall and describe its past? But when it comes to our past, it's all so mysterious. Most others rallied, albeit under difficult circumstances, and reconstituted their cultures even in this country. This shows strength and resilience of humanity. I refuse to believe that our strength is less than everyone else's. I know that we can catch hold of our psychological bearings and rise beyond the current disasters we're forced to face on a daily basis. Our will to survive must be stronger than our enemies will to destroy us, recognize this in our people's ancestry. Recognition stems from the word cognition which means the mental process by which the mind works and the world in which it works. We have this inherently (by nature, rather God), but we've allowed for ourselves to be taught in the ways of this Western Civilization, with all of its propaganda causing us to believe the worst about ourselves and each other.

Learning is merely the acquisition of knowledge not given beforehand. We're all born with a clean slated consciousness, but in this society it soon develops (rather under develops) into unconsciousness. We must become adept at thinking; this goes beyond memorizing information given. "Of all living organisms, humans are the most dependant on learning for their survival and   what they learn concerns both the physical and social environments in which they live." (Cultural anthropologist Robert Lavendo and Emily Schultz) The truth in this statement is obvious, but what's lacking is the recognition for humanity to be able to think independently; thinking is what sets us apart from most animals, which guided by instincts.

There often is a large gulf between what we see, and what we know and what we perceive and conceive. We may find ourselves frustrated with failures along the way, but we should receive it as a learning experience, because we will be destroyed if we don't make any attempts at raising the consciousness of our children. However, this can only be accomplished by our own consciousness being raised beyond that which it presently is.

To destroy a community, all that is needed is EXACTLY what we've received-disorder and desperation. Can anyone argue that the moment our ancestor's we're "emancipated," the plight of our people has virtually still been injustices by the government, mistreatment by financial institutions, erroneous teachings and a multitude of other negative effects. Our failure to pursue our destiny allows for others to mandate what we're to be, what we're to do, how to be it while we do it; for positive or negative. We constantly allow for others to control our lives, peers, political views, and propaganda from this media system. We must prove WHO WE ARE by what we do.

If we don't scrutinize the patterns that are in existence today, we'll continue to alienate ourselves from each other and God. Yet, with consciousness, we can stop harmful patterns, or at the very least begin to reverse them. The greater the victory is, simply means that a hard fought battle was (is) underway. Those who expect to benefit off of the blessings that consciousness will bring to our people MUST persevere and undergo the fatigue of supporting it. In order for something to work, it *must be* applied. All the consciousness in the world is irrelevant without the application of it.

There is a scripture in the Holy Bible which states, "Every purpose is established by counsel and with good advice makes war." (Proverbs 20 v. 11). We've all seen the residual effects of bad counsel which has lead up to bad wars; Iraqi invasion (both times) Afghanistan, just to name a couple.

We have to be unmoved by the numerous obstacles which will face us, internal and external, Persevere through them. A movement is considered worthy by the amount of sacrifice one is willing to make for it; liberty is unthinkable without risking self sacrifice.

"We were not created by God to be fearful, so cowardice will not preserve our heritage, in fact its cowardice today that is a chief culprit of our position. This cowardice has been caused by our unconsciousness." When a righteous cause arrives at its pivotal moment, all opposition that stands in front of it has no choice but to fall by the power behind it; this will not happen if we're not united.

Books are merely potential catalysts for action, so may we position ourselves to hear the truth as it is spoken, not to allow for such mindlessness. A deliberate behavior keeps us on the oath of destruction. If we truly love ourselves, we'll hate the fact that we're so divided. If we love the idea of liberty, we must fight against all who seek to see us continually constrained in bondage; physical or mental. "The basic tenets of black consciousness are that the black man must reject all value systems that seek to make him a foreigner in the country of his birth and reduces his basic human dignity." South African political prisoner Steven Biko.

May we consider the truths revealed and seek for the truths which are still hidden. This is the moment to advance our consciousness, because as hundreds of years have shown us, no one else is willing to.

This simply means that before any life altering decision, we must take time to discuss the ramifications for going forward, or we must consider the consequences for not progressing. I can think of no better way to end this than with a statement, so poignant, that it seems as if it was written last night and not over 40 years ago. "Black power ... is a call for black people in this country to unite, to recognize their heritage, to build a sense of community. It is a call for Black people to begin to define the question of our own goals, to lead their own organizations and support those organizations. It is a call to reject the racist institution and values of this society." (Stokely Carmicheal aka Kwame Toure)

Will we allow for the differences that we have to continue destroying us? Or will we allow for the things that we have in common to help us overcome the differences that we have? The question is yours alone to answer.

Subconsciously Unconscious

ABOUT THE AUTHOR

Marcos Gray is an ex-gang member who has sought enlightenment and aggressively pursues self education. Despite his incarceration, he has completed his GED course, and takes a variety of legal, Biblical and historical courses. This has been ongoing in an effort to increase his knowledge and effectiveness in his writings. The author realized that his previous lifestyle was detrimental to his future, his heritage and his community, thus becoming the main catalyst for his seeking and development of consciousness. The author also desires to raise the consciousness of those to whom he speaks for in the process of his own awareness. This is the author's first published work.